# Arts & Letters Apprentice

# Illustrated

by  Richard Hunt

ISBN 07457 0080 2

# Arts & Letters Apprentice

# Illustrated

Copyright 1992   Richard Hunt

## ISBN 07457 0080 2

Published by:

Kuma Computers Ltd
12 Horseshoe Park
Pangbourne
Berks
RG8 7JW
Tel 0734 844335
Fax 0734 844339

**Other Computing Titles From Kuma:**

**IBM PC & Compatible Micros**

| | |
|---|---|
| DTP Sourcebook - Fonts & Clip Art for the PC by J. L. Borman | 07457 0030 6 |
| PageMaker 4.0 for Windows by William B. Sanders | 07457 0031 4 |
| ZBasic Quick Reference Guide for PC & Mac by John Sumner | 07457 0140 X |
| The Windows Guide Book by Gill Gerhardi, Vic Gerhardi & Andy Berry | 07457 0041 1 |
| A Practical Guide to Timeworks Publisher 2 on the PC by Terry Freedman | 07457 0147 7 |
| The DR DOS 6 Quick Start Guide by John Sumner | 07457 0038 1 |
| Illustrated DR DOS 6 - The First 20 Hours by John Sumner | 07457 0044 6 |
| The User's Guide to Money Manager PC by John Sumner | 07457 0047 0 |
| Breaking Into Windows 3.1 by Bill Stott & Mark Brearley | 07457 0056 X |
| The Utter Novice Guide to GW Basic by Bill Aitken | 07457 0045 4 |
| The Utter Novice Guide to Q Basic by Bill Aitken | 07457 0046 2 |
| PagePlus Illustrated by Richard Hunt | 07457 0062 4 |
| DOS 5 Quick Start Guide by John Sumner | 07457 0054 3 |

**Commodore Amiga**

| | |
|---|---|
| Program Design Techniques for the Amiga by Paul Overaa | 07457 0032 2 |
| Intuition A Practical Programmers Guide by Mike Nelson | 07457 0143 4 |
| The Little Red Workbench 1.3 Book by Mark Smiddy | 07457 0048 9 |
| The Little Blue Workbench 2 Book by Mark Smiddy | 07457 0055 1 |

**Apple Macintosh**

| | |
|---|---|
| DTP Sourcebook - Fonts & Clip Art for the Mac by J. L. Borman | 07457 0050 0 |
| ZBasic Quick Reference Guide for PC & Mac by John Sumner | 07457 0140 X |
| The Quark Book by Rod Lawton & Isaac Davis | 07457 0052 7 |

**Psion Organiser**

| | |
|---|---|
| Psion Organiser Deciphered by Gill Gerhardi, Vic Gerhardi & Andy Berry | 07457 0139 6 |
| Using & Programming the Psion Organiser by Mike Shaw | 07457 0134 5 |
| File Handling on the Psion Organiser by Mike Shaw | 07457 0135 3 |
| Machine Code Programming on the Psion Organiser 2nd Ed. by Bill Aitken | 07457 0138 8 |
| Psion Organiser Comms Handbook by Gill & Vic Gerhardi & Andy Berry | 07457 0154 X |

**Psion Series 3**

| | |
|---|---|
| First Steps in Programming the Psion Series 3 by Mike Shaw | 07457 0145 0 |
| Serious Programming on the Psion Series 3 by Bill Aitken | 07457 0035 7 |

**Atari ST**

| | |
|---|---|
| Atari ST Explored 2nd Ed. by John Braga & Malcolm McMahon | 07457 0141 8 |
| Program Design Techniques for the Atari ST by Paul Overaa | 07457 0029 2 |
| Programming by Example - ST Basic by Dr. G. McMaster | 07457 0142 6 |
| A Practical Guide to Calamus Desktop Publishing by Terry Freedman | 07457 0159 0 |
| A Practical Guide to Timeworks on the Atari ST by Terry Freedman | 07457 0158 2 |

**Cambridge Z88**

| | |
|---|---|
| Z88 Magic by Gill Gerhardi, Vic Gerhardi & Andy Berry | 07457 0137 X |

**Games**

| | |
|---|---|
| Sega Megadrive Secrets by Rusel deMaria | 07457 0037 3 |
| Sega Megadrive Secrets Volume 2 by Rusel deMaria | 07457 0043 8 |
| Corish's Computer Games Guide | 07457 0150 7 |
| Awesome Sega Megadrive Secrets | 07457 0226 0 |

**Sharp IQ 7000 & 8000**

| | |
|---|---|
| Using Basic on the Sharp IQ by John Sumner | 07457 0034 9 |

**A selection from our fast-expanding range - latest full details on request**

# Contents

# Chapter 3. The Arts & Letters Menus Close Up

# Chapter 4. Objects

# Chapter 5. Symbols and Custom Libraries

# Chapter 6. Text

# Chapter 7. Working with Lines and Curves

# Chapter 8. Colours and Fills

# Introduction & Acknowledgements

## Introduction

*Arts & Letters Apprentice* is a graphics program which runs under Microsoft Windows 3.0 or 3.1 on the IBM and compatible PCs. *Apprentice* allows you to create graphics and artwork to print directly, for example posters and report covers, or to incorporate into DTP packages. You can easily modify the program's 3000+ pieces of clip-art or use them in your own designs. *Apprentice* has a good range of typefaces, sophisticated typographical controls and drawing tools. By using Windows printer drivers you get optimised printed results. And you get all this in a package which is (relatively) easy to use and reasonably priced.

What this book is intended to do is to provide an overview of the package and how to make use of its features, some ideas for using the program and to give useful references which are specific to *Arts & Letters Apprentice,* thus making the package easier and more enjoyable to use. Hopefully, some of the tips will be applicable to computer graphics in general.

## The Author

**Richard Hunt** is a freelance computer author and consultant. After taking degrees in European Business in Germany and England, he worked in

The Netherlands in publishing and marketing before turning to writing. Recent books include *PagePlus Illustrated* and (with Danny Kaye) *Skylight Illustrated*, also published by Kuma.

## Products and Trade names

*MS-DOS*, *Windows 3.0*, *Windows 3.1* and *Word for Windows 2.0* are products of Microsoft Corporation.
*Arts & Letters Apprentice* and *Arts & Letters Editor* are products of Computer Support Corporation, represented in the UK by The Roderick Manhattan Group.
*PostScript* is a trade name of Adobe Systems.
*Adobe Type Manager* is a product of Adobe Systems.
*Apple Mac* and *Macintosh* are trade names identifying products of Apple Computer.
*Ami Pro 3.0* is a product of Lotus Development.
*Paint Shop Pro* is a product of JASC Inc.
*PagePlus* is a product of Serif Inc.
*DR-DOS* is a product of Digital Research.

All other products and trade names not specifically mentioned are the property of their respective owners and are duly acknowledged.

## Acknowledgements

Thanks to everyone who helped to produce this book and in particular to Tom Towry and Amanda Adams at The Roderick Manhattan Group for their assistance and to Jon Day at Kuma.

Thanks to Margaret Busby for the cartoon at the start of the Appendices.

# Production Note

Camera-ready copy for this book was produced using Lotus Ami Pro 3.0 running on an Apricot Xen-S PC and printed to an Epson EPL-4300 laser printer. Screen images were grabbed from a standard VGA (640 x 480 pixels) monitor using *Paint Shop Pro* and LaserGo *GoScreen*.

# Before You Start...

## Assumptions

Throughout this book, several things are assumed. Firstly, that you have a PC with *Microsoft Windows* 3.0 or 3.1 and *Arts & Letters Apprentice 1.1* correctly installed on the hard disk; secondly, that you have a Windows-supported printer available; and thirdly that you are at least reasonably familiar with basic Windows commands. In particular, you should be happy using a mouse (or other pointing device such as a trackball) and be acquainted with the use of Windows' Clipboard feature. For information on installing and using Windows, refer to your Windows manual. You may wish to refer also to the Glossaries and other Appendices at the end of this book.

*Apprentice 1.1* has several enhancements over version 1.0. The most significant of these is the ability to convert solid objects to freeform objects, and to manipulate and view theStart/End points of freeform objects; object blending has also been added. There are over 100 new clip-art images, and the World Maps have been updated to September 1992.

If you are currently using *Apprentice 1.0*, contact the address on your warranty card for upgrade details.

## Conventions

For convenience, the program's full name is not always used. Instead, the shortened form *Apprentice* or the abbreviation *A&LE* is used.

Throughout this book, commands which you must type or keys which you must press are given in SMALL CAPITALS. Keys which must be pressed simultaneously are given in the form KEY1+KEY2; e.g. ALT+TAB means "press the Alt key and at the same time press the tab key, releasing them together". Keys which must be pressed consecutively are given in the form KEY1,KEY2; e.g. ALT,SPACEBAR means "press and release the Alt key, then press and release the spacebar".

Many commands in *Apprentice* can be accessed from a menu. "**Choose File/Save As...**" means "From the File Menu, choose the Save As... command".

# 1. What is Arts & Letters Apprentice?

## Graphics Programs

There are quite a number of Windows graphics programs available for the PC. They vary in type and sophistication, but all have at least two common features. One, they can save pictures in a recognised file format to be imported by other programs. Two, they can exchange data with other Windows programs via the clipboard.

### Paint Programs
Generally, there are two types of graphics program. Paint type programs are bitmap based, that is to say, they build up pictures by filling in the squares of a grid. This results in an image made up of many tiny dots, or pixels. Enlarging bitmaps can cause problems; the edge of the graphic may appear jagged or the ugly Moiré effect may be evident. The most widely know paint type program is probably the Paintbrush accessory supplied with Windows. PCX, BMP, MSP and TIF are four common types of bitmap image file supported by many applications.

### Draw Programs
Draw type programs on the other hand build up pictures with lines from point *a* to point *b* and with hollow shapes which contain a coloured fill pattern.

7

Because they are basically mathematical descriptions of vectors, draw type graphics are less prone to distortion when they are resized than bitmaps. Often, a bitmap can be used as a part of a design in a draw program. WMF (Windows Metafiles) and CGM (Computer Graphics Metafiles) are two well-known vector formats.

Unlike paint packages, draw packages work in layers. Each object is on its own layer and can be moved from the 'front' to the 'back' or to intermediate layers, and can be partially hidden by or used to hide other objects. New objects are always added at the 'front' of a page.

## Presentation Graphics Programs

Presentation Graphics programs are usually used to create special effects with data from other applications, e.g. spreadsheets, with a view to making charts or diagrams which can be used for reports, output as overhead projector slides or even 35mm slides. *Apprentice* can do this as well as acting as a conventional drawing program.

It's a useful facility, especially if you don't have one of the newer spreadsheets with built-in charting, or for making average figures look really special.

## Apprentice specifics

*Apprentice* is basically a draw-type program which stores information in its own GED (*Graphic Environment Document)* file format; although it can import and export files in a variety of both bitmap and vector formats. (Appendix D, *Apprentice Import & Export Filters* contains a full list.)

*Apprentice* uses an object-based approach. Everything placed on the screen - text, bitmaps, freeform lines and shapes, clip-art or predefined symbols - is an object which can be manipulated in various ways. The idea is that the user can arrange combinations of objects to create the desired effect, for example by placing a group of symbols and descriptive text on a coloured background.

*Apprentice* and its big brother, the *Arts & Letters Graphics Editor* can do something which many other graphics programs cannot do: they can combine bitmap and draw type graphics in one design. This enables you, for example, to scan a photograph, import it into *Apprentice* and add Clip-Art symbols to create special design effects. Or, you could draw an original by hand, scan it into a bitmap format, import it into *Apprentice*, add decorations and then save the whole design as a GED file.

## Clip-Art

Clip-Art is the name given to predrawn collections of pictures mainly for use with Graphics and Desktop Publishing (DTP) programs. There is a lot of Clip-Art around, either in the form of bitmap images which have been scanned from hand-drawn or printed artwork or draw-type graphics drawn expressly with a computer drawing package. It has to be said that much of the available Clip-Art, particularly scanned bitmaps, is of indifferent quality. On the other hand, some of the high-quality draw-type Clip-Art costs a lot of money. *Apprentice* however includes over 3000 outline Clip-Art symbols, many of them in full colour, which you can either use 'as-is' or modify and incorporate in your own designs. Details of the *Apprentice* Clip-Art are contained in the *Arts & Letters Apprentice Clip Art Handbook.*

## Apprentice and other Windows programs

*Apprentice* can communicate with other Windows programs in two ways. Firstly, a complete design can be saved as a graphics file - exported, in *Apprentice* terms - in one of several formats and the saved file can then be imported for use by another program. Conversely, *Apprentice* can import a file saved by another program. Secondly, objects from *Apprentice* or even a whole design can be placed on the Windows Clipboard and pasted into another application, or the reverse process can be carried out, pasting from the Clipboard into *Apprentice*. This is very useful if neither program has any common file format.

# 2. The Arts & Letters Apprentice Screen and Tools

## Overview

Like any other Windows application, you usually start *Apprentice* by double-clicking on its icon in the program manager. During run up, the program

displays a copyright screen. This screen can also be accessed during an *Apprentice* session by clicking on **Help/About**.

By default, Arts & Letters *Apprentice* opens with the screen maximised, that is occupying the whole of the monitor.

The screen initially does not display the rulers, and until you use **File/Printer Setup..** (or unless you change the default settings) the page will not be

11

formatted for any particular printer. The *Apprentice* screen displays the usual Windows Title Bar, Menu Bar, System Bar, Minimize/Maximize buttons and scroll bars, as well as its own features which are described below.

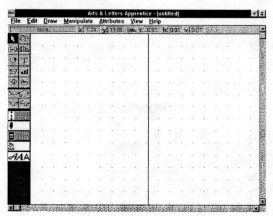

## The Title Bar and Menu Bar

The Title Bar displays the program title, followed [in square brackets] by the name of the GED file which is in use. If the file has not yet been saved, the display reads [untitled].

The Menu Bar contains the names of the *Apprentice*

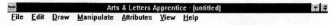

menus. There are seven menus - **File**, **Edit**, **Draw**, **Manipulate**, **Attributes**, **View** and **Help**. Each menu contains choices which either issue a command, access a sub menu with further options or bring up a dialog box to specify detailed options. To access a menu, either click on its title with the mouse pointer or press the ALT key followed by the underlined letter in the menu's name (for example ALT, F will access the File menu; ALT, V the View menu, and so on).

Choosing **View/Full Screen** or using the CTRL+X keyboard shortcut turns display of the Title Bar and Menu Bar off and on.

### The Status Bar

The Status Bar is below the Menu Bar. It displays (from left to right) the reference number of the

selected symbol (or the name of a piece of clip art), the co-ordinates of the mouse pointer on the page, the degree of rotation and the degrees of horizontal and vertical slant.

It also displays other messages according to which operation is being carried out. It can be turned off by unchecking the Status check box in the Viewing Preferences dialog.

# The Toolbox

The toolbox is located at the left of the screen, below the Status Bar. It contains general tools for drawing and manipulating objects, line drawing and editing tools, line and fill colour tools, as well as line, fill and text attribute tools. The toolbox can be turned off by unchecking the Toolbox check box in the

Viewing Preferences dialog accessed by choosing **View/Preferences....**.

## General Tools

The tools are displayed in a block of ten icons at the top of the toolbox. Some of them duplicate functions which can also be accessed by menu or keyboard shortcut commands.

### The Pointer

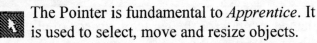 The Pointer is fundamental to *Apprentice*. It is used to select, move and resize objects.

When in freeform editing mode, the pointer changes to a triangular arrowhead which is used to add, select, delete and move handles.

### The Symbol Tool

Clicking on the Symbol Tool brings up the Add Symbol dialog, which can also be accessed by choosing **Draw/Symbol...** or keyboard shortcut CTRL+S.

### The Duplicate Tool

When the Duplicate Tool is selected, the cursor changes to a series of boxes linked by an arrow. Dragging on a selected object will create a duplicate of it. Duplication can also be selected by choosing **Manipulate/Duplicate** or using the keyboard shortcut CTRL+D.

### The Library Tool

 The Library Tool provides quick access to the Clip-art manager. The Clip-art manager can also be accessed by choosing **Draw/Clip-art manager...** or using the keyboard shortcut CTRL+C.

### The Rotate Tool

 The Rotate tool is used to rotate selected object(s) clockwise or anti-clockwise and to move the centre of rotation. The status bar shows how much the object has been rotated by.

### The Text Tool

 Clicking on the Text Tool brings up the text entry/editing dialog, if no object is selected. If a text object is selected, the text entry/editing dialog is brought up to enable you to alter the selected text. Text entry/editing can also be accessed by using **Draw/Text...** or the keyboard shortcut CTRL+T.

### The Slant Tool

 The Slant Tool is used to apply a slant effect to selected objects and to move the slant effect's pivot point.

### The Chart Tool

 Clicking on the Chart Tool accesses *Apprentice*'s charting features. Chart drawing can also be accessed from the menus by choosing **Draw/Chart**.

### The Zoom Tool

 When the Zoom Tool is selected, the mouse pointer changes to a magnifying glass. Click and drag on the page to zoom in on a particular area. The Zoom Tool can also be accessed by choosing **View/Zoom In** or by using the keyboard shortcut CTRL+Z.

### The Block Select Tool

 When the Block Select Tool is selected, the mouse pointer changes to a pointing finger. Click and drag to draw a rectangle enclosing one or more objects to create a temporary block of objects which can then be moved and manipulated as one item. The Block Select Tool can also be selected by choosing **Edit/Block Select** or by using the keyboard shortcut CTRL+B.

## The Freeform Tools

The three freeform drawing tools are located in the toolbox in a block below the main tools at the left of the screen.

### Edit Freeform

 Click on the Edit Freeform tool to begin editing a freeform line or curve which has been drawn using *Apprentice*'s line drawing tools or a shape which has been converted from a solid object to a freeform object using **Draw/Cvt to Freeform**. Clicking on this tool has the same effect as choosing **Draw/Edit Freeform**, or the keyboard shortcut CTRL+P. Clicking the right mouse button leaves freeform editing mode.

### Draw Line

The Line Draw tool is used for drawing straight lines. Clicking on this tool has the same effect as choosing **Draw/Line** or using the shortcut F2 key. Clicking on the *right* mouse button straight after drawing a line enters Line Edit mode.

### Draw Curve

The Draw Curve tool is used for drawing curved lines. Clicking on this tool has the same effect as choosing **Draw/Curve** or the shortcut F3 key. Clicking on the *right* mouse button straight after drawing a curve enters Line Edit mode.

## The Attribute Tools

### The Line Color Tool

The Line Color Tool accesses a dialog for changing a line's colour attributes. The colour attributes dialog can also be accessed by choosing **Attributes/Color...**.

### The Line Attributes Tool

The Line Attributes Tool accesses the Line Attributes Dialog. This can also be accessed by choosing **Attributes/Line...** or by using the keyboard shortcut CTRL+L. The line in the tool shows the current line type, width and colour if no object is selected; if an object is selected it shows that object's line attributes.

### The Fill Color Tool

The Fill Color Tool accesses a dialog for changing a fill's colour attributes. The fill colour dialog can also be accessed by choosing **Attributes/Color...**.

### The Fill Attributes Tool

Clicking on the Fill Attributes Tool accesses the Fill Attributes dialog. This can also be accessed by choosing **Attributes/Fill...** or by using the keyboard shortcut CTRL+I. A representation of either the current fill style or the currently selected object's fill style is shown in the Tool.

### The Type Attributes Tool

Clicking on the Type Attributes Tool accesses the Type Attributes dialog. This can also be accessed by choosing **Attributes/Type...** or by the keyboard shortcut CTRL+Y.

## Setting Apprentice Defaults

*Apprentice* stores the values which it uses at startup to set the items which are displayed, grid size, ruler units, fill style and colour, default typeface etc. in a .DEF file. The DEF file can also set up a particular page size and precision and a default printer, so that you don't have to set up the page and printer at the start of every session.The DEF file set up during installation, which *Apprentice* uses automatically, is called STARTUP.DEF, which you may not like.

There are two possible ways round this:

> *create a new DEF file and make Apprentice use it*
> *overwrite STARTUP.DEF.*

Creating a new definition file is easy. First, make the screen appear as you want it to. Choose **View/Preferences...** to bring up the Viewing preferences dialog, and set the display as you want. Close this dialog and change the line, fill and color attributes as described earlier. You might also use **File/Printer Setup...** to setup your usual printer.

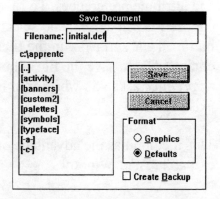

To save the changes, choose **File/Save As...** and select the Defaults radio button. Type a filename, for example INITIAL.DEF in the filename box. Then click on OK to carry out the save.

*Apprentice* knows which .DEF file to use because the `apprentice config` line in the [a&l] section of WIN.INI tells it. As first installed this line reads:

```
apprentice config=C:\APPRENTC\STARTUP.DEF
```

If you want *Apprentice* to start up using another .DEF file you must alter this line to read (for example)

```
apprentice config=C:\APPRENTC\INITIAL.DEF
```

After altering WIN.INI, you must exit and restart Windows so that the new WIN.INI takes effect. When you next start *Apprentice*, the new DEF file will be used.

The other method, overwriting the existing STARTUP.DEF, is simpler. Set your view, printer, page and attribute preferences. To save the changes, choose **File/Save As...** and select the Defaults radio button. Type SETUP.DEF in the filename box. Then click on OK to save the file. Choose OK when *Apprentice* asks you whether or not to overwrite the existing file.

This method has the advantage of not needing to exit and restart Windows.

# 3. The Arts & Letters Apprentice Menus Close-up

## Overview

The menus provide access to *Apprentice* commands and dialogs. Most of the time, it is easier to use the mouse pointer and the tools, but there are certain functions which can only be carried out from the menus.

### The File Menu

The File Menu contains commands related to filing and printing operations.

**File/New** allows you to abandon the current design and start a new one on a blank page. If there is unsaved or changed work on the screen, *Apprentice* will prompt you as to whether to save the changes or not before starting a new design document.

**File/Open...** brings up a normal Windows filing dialog with a list of previously saved GED files which can be loaded for viewing or editing if the Graphics radio button is selected. To load a GED file, either double-click on its name in the list box or highlight its name in the list box and click on the Open button. If the As New Document check box is

21

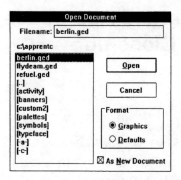

checked, the design currently displayed will be cleared first; if the box is unchecked, the selected GED file will be placed on top of the currently displayed design (Merged).

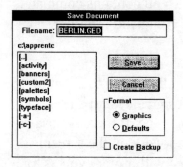

**File/Save As...** brings up a standard Windows filing dialog where a design can be given a name to save it under. Type the new name in the Filename box. *Apprentice* will add the .GED extension automatically. If you try to save a new design with an existing name, *Apprentice* will ask whether you wish to overwrite the existing file. Checking the Create Backup box will automatically create backup copies of your work at the cost of using more disk space.

22

**File/Save** (keyboard shortcut F9) saves the current modifications to a named design. If an attempt is made to Save an untitled design, the Save As... dialog is displayed.

**File/Page Setup...** brings up a dialog where you can

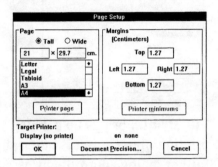

specify the page size and orientation. This should be the same as the paper used by the type of printer which you have specified with **Printer Setup**. Clicking on the Printer Page and Printer Minimums buttons sets the page up to match the printer's default values automatically.

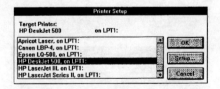

**File/Printer Setup...** brings up a dialog where you can select a printer to send output to. If you change the printer to one whose page sizes do not match those specified in the **Page Setup...** dialog you will

be asked whether you wish to change the page
setup.

**File/Print...** brings up a dialog which controls
printing options. If a PostScript printer is selected, a
further dialog controlling PostScript options can be
accessed by clicking on the Setup button, which is
important if you are sending work to a service
bureau for output via an imagesetter on bromide or
as film. Clicking on the Print button starts the
printing process; clicking on the To File button
directs the output to a file rather than the printer
port.

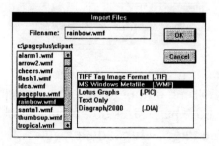

*The Import filing
dialog allows you
to select import
options*

**File/Import** brings up a Windows filing dialog where you can select files in various formats, created by other programs, to import for use in *Apprentice*. To import a file, highlight the appropriate file type in the file type list and either highlight the filename in the file list and click on the OK button, or double-click on the filename in the file list.

**File/Export** brings up a Windows filing dialog which controls *Apprentice*'s export features. You

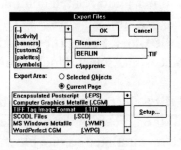

can choose to export either selected objects or whole pages created with *Apprentice* in various file formats for use by other programs. Clicking on the Setup... button brings up a dialog where you can specify the export options for each format.There is a different setup dialog for each export format; details of the options are given in Appendix D, *Apprentice Import & Export Filters*.

**File/Exit** exits *Apprentice*. If there is unsaved or changed work on the screen, *Apprentice* will prompt you as to whether or not to save the changes.

## The Edit Menu

The Edit Menu contains commands related to selecting and deleting objects, and controls *Apprentice*'s interaction with the Windows Clipboard.

**Edit/Undelete** allows you to restore an accidentally deleted object. According to the last operation carried out, this may appear as **Undo Attribute** or another undo related command.

**Edit/Block Select** (keyboard shortcut CTRL+B) places the Select Block Tool on the screen.

**Edit/Select All** (keyboard shortcut CTRL+A) selects all the objects in the document and allows them to be manipulated as one block.

**Edit/Deselect All** deselects all currently selected objects.

**Edit/Cut** (keyboard shortcut SHIFT+DEL) cuts the selected object(s) from the document and places them onto the Windows Clipboard.

**Edit/Copy** (keyboard shortcut CTRL+INS) places a copy of the selected object(s) from the document onto the Windows Clipboard.

**Edit/Paste** (keyboard shortcut SHIFT+INS) places a copy of whatever is on the Clipboard into *Apprentice*.

**Edit/Paste Options** ➤ brings up a sub menu where you can choose whether pasted items are pasted on top of or below other items.

**Edit/Clipboard...** brings up a dialog which you can use to set clipboard options.

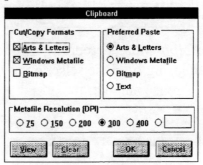

**Edit/Clear** (keyboard shortcut DEL) deletes the selected object(s) from the document.

## The Draw Menu

The Draw Menu contains commands related to adding Symbols Clip-art objects, and text to *Apprentice* designs. It is also the menu from which to access freeform drawing and editing features, including conversion of Symbols to freeform objects, Chart drawing and the Activity Manager.

27

Finally the Draw menu contains the snapping controls.

**Draw/Symbol...** (keyboard shortcut CTRL+S) brings up the Symbol dialog which allows you to add one

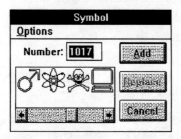

of *Apprentice*'s predrawn symbols to the design by choosing from the selection or by entering a symbol reference number.

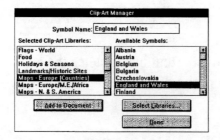

**Draw/Clip-Art Manager...** (keyboard shortcut CTRL+C) brings up the Clip-Art Manager dialog, from which you can select a piece of predrawn Clip-Art from the selected Custom Library to add to your document.

**Draw/Text...** brings up the text entry and editing

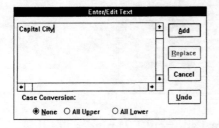

*The text entry and editing dialog*

box, where you can enter or edit text to be included in an *Apprentice* design.

**Draw/Chart...** accesses *Apprentice*'s chart drawing

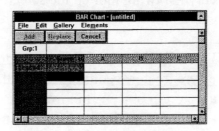

facilities. Using the chart drawing features it is possible to create spectacular charts. The Chart drawing facilities run semi-independently in the Chart Window which has its own menus (described in Chapter 10).

**Draw/Activity Manager...** brings up the Activity Manager dialog where you can access a variety of activities (e.g. tutorials, sample .GED files, text effects).

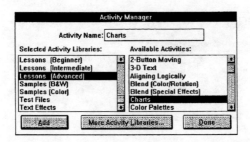

**Draw/Line** (keyboard shortcut F2) places the line drawing tool on the screen ready to draw a straight line.

**Draw/Curve** (keyboard shortcut F3) places the curve drawing tool on the screen ready to draw a curve.

**Draw/Edit Freeform** (keyboard shortcut CTRL+P) enters freeform editing mode if the selected object is a freeform object. If in freeform editing mode already, this exits freeform editing mode.

**Draw/Cvt to Freeform** (keyboard shortcut F8) converts a selected non-freeform object (e.g. a typeface character or predefined symbol) into a freeform object which can then be edited.

**Draw/Add Handle** (keyboard shortcut F5) changes the mouse pointer to the handle-adding tool. Clicking the handle-adding tool on a freeform object adds an extra handle.

**Draw/Join Open Shapes** (keyboard shortcut F7) joins two open shapes which have been selected with SHIFT+CLICK into one open shape.

**Draw/Set Start/End Point** allows you to specify the start and end points of a closed freeform shape.

**Draw/Shape Info...** brings up a dialog which

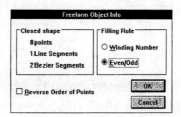

displays information about how a freeform object is made up.

**Draw/Snap To ➤**brings up a sub menu where you can specify whether objects snap to the snapping grid or points.

**Draw/Snap Options...** brings up a dialog where you can specify the snapping options. Increasing the

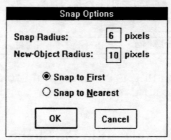

Snap Radius value makes Apprentice carry out more smoothing on freehand curves.

## The Manipulate Menu

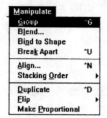

The Manipulate Menu contains commands relating to aligning objects on the page, making and breaking up groups of objects, applying blend effects, binding text to a freeform object and duplicating objects.

**Manipulate/Group** (keyboard shortcut CTRL+G) groups a block of selected objects into a permanent group.

**Manipulate/Blend...** brings up a dialog where you can specify the parameters for a blend operation.

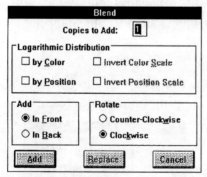

Blending is covered in more detail in the chapter on Special Effects.

**Manipulate/Bind to Shape...** brings up a dialog where you can set the options for binding a piece of

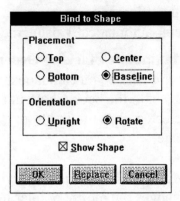

text to a freeform object. Binding text to a shape is covered in detail in the chapter on Special Effects.

**Manipulate/Break Apart** (keyboard shortcut CTRL+U) breaks apart (ungroups) Groups of objects created with **Manipulate/Group** or breaks apart Clip-Art or freeform objects.

**Manipulate/Align...** (keyboard shortcut CTRL+N) brings up a dialog which allows you to specify the

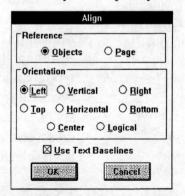

vertical and horizontal alignment of objects. Objects can be aligned with reference to the page or to each other. Some Symbols can be aligned semi-automatically using the Logical option.

**Manipulate/Stacking Order** ➤ accesses a sub menu where you can choose to send the selected object to the back (shortcut CTRL+K) or bring the selected object to the front (shortcut CTRL+F) of the page.

**Manipulate/Duplicate** (keyboard shortcut CTRL+D) changes the mouse pointer into the Duplicate Tool.

**Manipulate/Flip** accesses a sub menu where you can choose to Flip (mirror) the selected object(s) Vertically or Horizontally.

**Manipulate/Make Proportional** restores a selected object to its original aspect ratio.

## The Attributes Menu

| Attributes | |
|---|---|
| Color... | |
| Fill... | ^I |
| Line... | ^L |
| Type... | ~Y |
| Styles... | |
| Save | ^Q |
| Recall | ^R |

The Attributes Menu contains commands relating to the colour, fill and line style of all objects. Additionally, for text objects, typographic controls can be accessed from this menu. The fill styles and colours will be shown on screen unless Outline View has been selected.

**Attributes/Color...** brings up a dialog where you can specify the fill and/or line colour of selected objects. The default colour palette has eight colours:

34

more named palettes can be appended or substituted and new colours mixed using the commands in dialog's Options and File menus. This dialog can also be made to remain visible.

**Attributes/Fill...** (keyboard shortcut CTRL+I) displays a dialog for changing the interior fill of an

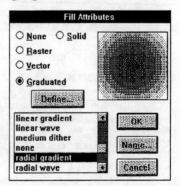

object. There are several predefined styles, and you can define new styles or modify existing ones.

**Attributes/Line...** (keyboard shortcut CTRL+L) brings up a dialog where you can change the width and pattern of a selected object's lines. The Define...

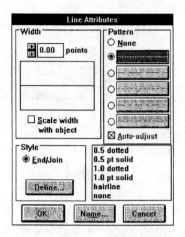

button leads to a further dialog where you can specify line end and join styles.

**Attributes/Type...** (keyboard shortcut CTRL+Y) brings up a dialog where you can specify the

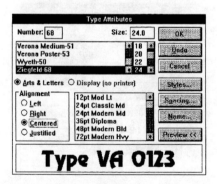

typeface, size, style and spacing of text. Buttons lead to dialogs with further typographic controls.

**Attributes/Styles** brings up a dialog where you can choose a standard attribute to apply to selected object(s), or create a new style. This menu option

extent duplicates parts of the three dialogs described above.

**Attributes/Save** (keyboard shortcut CTRL+Q) saves the colour, fill, line, and type attributes of the currently selected object.

**Attributes/Recall** (keyboard shortcut CTRL+R) applies the attributes stored with **Attributes/Save** to a selected object.If no attributes have been stored, the current attributes are applied.

## The View Menu

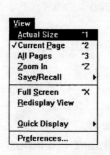

The View Menu contains commands relating to the way in which you view the page and the objects on it. You can choose to view the page at various sizes, turn display of screen items on or off and also specify how objects should be displayed (e.g. full colour or wireframe).

**View/Actual Size** (keyboard shortcut CTRL+1) zooms to display the selected object at actual size.

**View/Current Page** (keyboard shortcut CTRL+2) zooms to display the whole of the current page.

**View/All Pages** (keyboard shortcut CTRL+3) zooms to display all the pages of the current document.

**View/Zoom In** (keyboard shortcut CTRL+z) changes the mouse pointer into the Zoom Tool.

**View/Save/Recall** ➤ accesses a sub menu with three options:
**Previous** (keyboard shortcut CTRL+v) returns you to the previous page display;
**Save** saves the current page display;
**Recall** recalls the page display saved with **View/Save/Save**.

**View/Full Screen** (keyboard shortcut CTRL+k) turns off display of the Title Bar and the Menu Bar.

**View/Redisplay View** forces a screen redraw.

**View/Control Points** (keyboard shortcut CTRL+4) turns the display of curve control points on and off. When in Freeform Editing mode, and a handle on a freeform curve is selected, choosing this command displays the handle's control points, which can then be dragged to adjust the curve.

**View/Quick Display** ➤ accesses a sub menu with display options.

**Outlines Only** (keyboard shortcut CTRL+6) makes *Apprentice* display only the wireframe outlines of objects and not their fills or actual line widths.

**Gradients** ➤displays a further submenu controlling whether and how gradients should be displayed.
**Show Fills** turns the display of fills on or off.
**Show WideLines** turns the display of actual width lines on and off.
**Bitmaps** turns the display of imported or pasted bitmaps on and off.

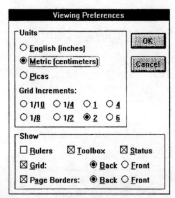

**View/Preferences...** displays a dialog where you can specify your preferences for *Apprentice*'s display during the current session. Rulers, the Toolbox, the Status Bar, the grid and page edges can be set not to display, and you can also alter the measurement units and grid spacing.

## The Help Menu

The Help Menu allows you to access the *Apprentice* Help system. The *Apprentice* help system is a standard Windows Help system.

**Help/Help For Help...** displays general instructions on using Windows Help.

**Help/Help for Items** (keyboard shortcut F1) displays context-sensitive help. In Help for Items mode, the mouse cursor displays as a pointer with a question mark beside it. Click on an item with the Help pointer to view Help for that item. If context-sensitive help is not available for the chosen item, an information message is displayed.

**Help/Help Index...** leads to Apprentice Help's index.

**Help/About...** displays the *Apprentice* information screen.

# 4. Objects

## Overview

Every item which you place or draw on the page is an object. Objects can be manipulated, rotated, slanted and have various fill styles and line styles applied to them.

If you have chosen to display the Status Bar, it will show a message describing the currently selected object(s). The descriptive message appears at the left of the status bar and can be: the reference # of a symbol, the name of piece of Clip Art (e.g. G.>MIG21), a named group from a piece of Clip Art which has been broken apart (e.g. G>Labels), or the status of a freeform object (e.g. open shape or closed shape).

## Types of Object

### Solid Objects
Solid objects have fixed outlines. When placed into a document, *Apprentice* symbols are solid objects. Text, as first placed into *Apprentice*, is also regarded as a solid object.

### Freeform Objects
Freeform objects have outlines which can be changed by using *Apprentice*'s freeform editing features. Freeform objects can be either Open Shapes, such as lines and simple or elaborate curves

41

where the ends do not meet; or Closed Shapes such as lines or curves which have ends that meet. A solid object can be converted into a freeform object using **Draw/Cvt to Freeform**. Freeform objects are more flexible than solid objects. For example, you can make text run around or along the outline of a freeform object.

# Selecting Objects

Before an object can be manipulated or moved, it must be selected. Objects can be selected either as single objects or as multiple objects.

## Single objects

To select a single object, choose the pointer tool from the toolbox. Position the pointer over the desired object and click the mouse button or press the spacebar. When an object is selected, handles

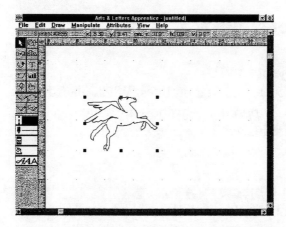

appear at its corners and edge midpoints.

## Multiple Objects

Multiple objects can be selected (as in other Windows programs) using the pointer and SHIFT+CLICK.

Select the first object as described above. Hold down the SHIFT key, position the pointer over the next object and click the mouse button. Repeat this step until all the desired objects have been selected. The number of objects in the multiple will be shown

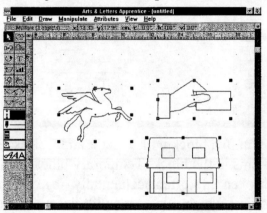

in the status bar, and a set of handles will appear on each object.

## Multiple Objects - Blocks

There are two ways to select a block. To select all the items on a page, choose **Edit/Select All** (keyboard CTRL+A). To select all the objects inside a rectangular area, choose the Block Select Tool from the Toolbox or choose **Edit/Block Select** (keyboard shortcut CTRL+B) and using the tool draw a rectangle around all the objects which you wish to select. You must draw a rectangle which completely encloses all the desired objects: if an object isn't wholly within the rectangle, it won't be included in the block. One set of handles will appear around the whole block.

A block is a temporary group. Clicking on any one

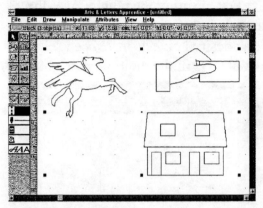

item in a block will select it and 'release' the other items in the block. Temporary blocks can be easily broken up - often accidentally - by clicking on one object which selects it and 'releases' the other objects.

## Multiple Objects - Groups

Because it's so easy to break blocks up accidentally, it's often better to convert blocks into permanent groups by choosing **Manipulate/Group** (keyboard shortcut CTRL+G).

A permanent group cannot be broken apart unintentionally by clicking on one of its elements; you must choose **Manipulate/Break Apart** (keyboard shortcut CTRL+U).

# Duplicating Objects

The quickest way of copying an object is to use the
Duplicate Tool. Firstly, choose the Duplicate Tool

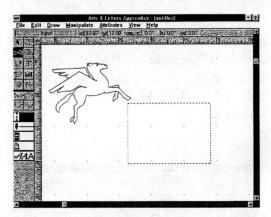

from the Toolbox. The pointer changes to the
Duplicate Tool. Click and drag on the object which
you wish to copy. You will see a dashed outline
being dragged. This outline represents the new
object - the copy. When you release the button, the
new object will be displayed properly.

If you drag on a corner handle, the copy (the new
object) will be a different size to the original, but
with its aspect ratio maintained. If you drag on an
edge handle, the copy will be a different size but
with its aspect ratio distorted.

Copying an object using the Duplicate Tool does
not involve use of the Windows Clipboard and can
therefore be a lot faster than using **Edit/Copy** and
**Edit/Paste**.

## Duplicating using the keyboard

To duplicate an object using the keyboard, place the Duplicate Tool on the main part of the object. Press and hold down the spacebar. A dashed outline appears representing the new object. Still holding down the spacebar, move the outline up with the Up arrow, left with the Left arrow, right with the Right arrow or down with the Down arrow. When you have finished moving the new object, release the spacebar.

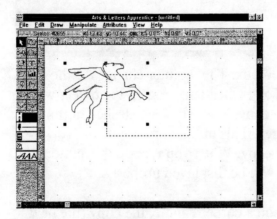

# Moving Objects

To move an object, place the pointer over the main part of the object (*not* the handles). Press and hold down the left button to 'pick up' the object. A dashed outline representing the object's bounding box becomes visible. Drag the pointer, releasing the left button when the object's dashed outline is

over the object's desired new position. The object
will then be displayed properly again.

## Moving objects using the keyboard

It's often easier to move objects accurately with the
keyboard than with the mouse.To move an object
exactly horizontally or vertically, select it as normal
by clicking on it. Place the pointer on the main part
of the object, but do not hold the button down.
Press and hold down the spacebar. A dashed outline
appears around the object. Still holding down the
spacebar, move the object up with the Up arrow, left
with the Left arrow, right with the Right arrow or
down with the Down arrow. When you have
finished moving the object, release the spacebar.

Multiples selected with SHIFT+CLICK cannot be
moved as one object - Blocks selected with the
Block Select tool and Groups however can be.

# Resizing Objects

To resize an object, place the pointer over one of
the object's handles. Press and hold down the left
button. The object is surrounded by a dashed
outline. Drag the pointer, releasing the button when
the object's dashed outline is the same as the desired
new size. The object will then be displayed at its
new size.

47

Dragging on a corner handle will resize the object proportionally. Dragging on an edge handle will resize the object without keeping it in proportion.

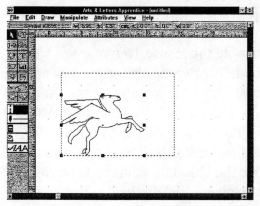

## Resizing objects using the keyboard

It's easier to make fine movements with the keyboard controls rather than the mouse. To resize an object using the keyboard, select it as normal by clicking on it. Place the pointer on one of the object's handles. Press and hold down the spacebar. A dashed outline appears around the object. Still holding down the spacebar, resize the outline using the arrow keys. When the outline is the size you want, release the spacebar. Moving the outline using a corner handle will resize the object proportionally. Moving the outline using an edge handle will resize the object without keeping it in proportion.

Multiples selected with SHIFT+CLICK cannot be resized as one object, but blocks selected with the Block Select Tool can be. During resizing, the

48

width and height of the selected object are given in the status bar.

# Rotating Objects

To rotate an object, first of all select it. Choose the Rotate Tool from the toolbox. The pointer changes

to a small arrow with a rotation symbol.[↻ ] The centre of rotation appears as a cross hair on a circle at the centre of the object. It can be moved by dragging it with the Rotate Tool. Rotate the object by dragging on one of its corner handles with the rotate tool. The amount of rotation (in degrees) is

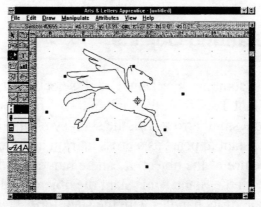

shown in the Status Bar after the r:. Clicking the right button leaves rotation mode.

## Rotating objects using the keyboard

You may find it easier to make fine movements with the keyboard controls rather than the mouse. To rotate an object with greater control over the degree of rotation, select it as normal by clicking on it. Choose the Rotate Tool and place the tool's pointer on one of the corner handles, but do not hold the button down. Press and hold down the spacebar. A dashed outline appears around the object. Still holding down the spacebar, rotate the object anticlockwise with the Up or Left arrow keys, or clockwise with the Right or Down arrow keys. The amount of rotation (in degrees) is shown in the Status Bar after the r:. When you have finished rotating the object, release the spacebar.

Multiples selected with SHIFT+CLICK cannot be rotated, but Blocks selected with the Block Select Tool and Groups can be.

## Slanting Objects

To slant an object, first of all select it. Choose the Slant Tool from the toolbox. The pointer changes to a small arrow with the slant symbol. The centre of slant appears as a cross hair on a circle at the centre of the object. It can be moved by dragging it with the Slant Tool. Slant the object by dragging on one of its handles with the slant tool. The amount of slant (in degrees) is shown in the Status Bar after the h: and v:. Clicking the right button leaves slant mode.

### Slanting objects using the keyboard
You may find it easier to make fine movements with the keyboard controls rather than the mouse. To

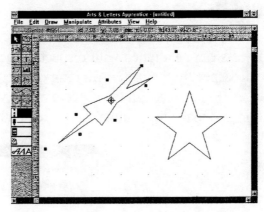

slant an object with greater control over the degree
of slant, select it as normal by clicking on it. Choose
the Slant Tool and place the tool's pointer on one of
the corner handles, but do not hold the button
down. Press and hold down the spacebar. A dashed
outline appears around the object. Still holding
down the spacebar, slant the object vertically with
the Up or Down arrow keys, or horizontally with the
Right or Left arrow keys. The amount of vertical
and/or horizontal slant (in degrees) is shown in the
Status Bar after the h: and v:. When you have
finished slanting the object, release the spacebar.

Multiples composed of individually selected objects
(selected with SHIFT+CLICK) cannot be slanted, but
Blocks selected with the Block Select Tool and
Groups can be.

51

# Aligning Objects

Objects can be aligned with respect to each other or with respect to the page. Aligning objects has two stages. First, select all the objects which you wish to align and make them into a multiple or a block.

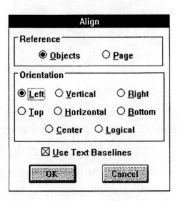

Using the pointer tool and shift-clicking the left button is usually the best way of doing this. Next, choose **Manipulate/Align...** or use the CTRL+N keyboard shortcut to bring up the Align Items dialog. From the dialog, choose how you wish to align the items by selecting the appropriate radio button. Radio buttons are used to make 'either/or' choices: you can choose Reference to Objects or Reference to Page but not both. The tables below show the effects of the various options.

## With reference to Objects:

| Choice | Effect |
|--------|--------|
| Left | Aligns objects so that their left edges are in |

| Choice | Effect |
| --- | --- |
| | line with the leftmost selected object |
| Vertical | Aligns objects so that their centres are in a vertical line |
| Right | Aligns objects so that their right edges line up with the right edge of the rightmost selected object |
| Top | Aligns the objects with their top edges level with the top edge of the topmost selected object |
| Horizontal | Aligns objects so that their centres are in a horizontal line |
| Bottom | Aligns the objects with their bottom edges level with the bottom edge of the bottom-most object |
| Center | Aligns the objects with their centre-points at the same position |
| Logical | Aligns certain combinations of symbols logically |
| Use text baselines | If checked, uses the text baseline as the bottom of a text group. If unchecked, uses the bottom handles of a text group as the bottom |

# With reference to Pages:

| Choice | Effect |
| --- | --- |
| Left | Aligns objects with their left edges at the left of the current page |
| Vertical | Aligns objects with their centres in a vertical line down the middle of the page |
| Right | Aligns objects with their right edges at the right of the current page |
| Top | Aligns the objects with their top edges at the top of the current page |
| Horizontal | Aligns objects so that their centres are in a horizontal line across the middle of the page |
| Bottom | Aligns the objects with their bottom edges level at the bottom of the current page |

| Choice | Effect |
|---|---|
| Center | Aligns the objects with their centre-points at the centre of the page |
| Logical | Aligns certain combinations of symbols logically on the page |
| Use text baselines | If checked, uses the text baseline as the bottom of a text group. If unchecked, uses the bottom handles of a text group as the bottom |

## Using Logical Alignment

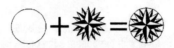

Certain combinations of symbols can be aligned automatically. For example, accents can be added to a basic symbol, such as adding a multi-pointed star to a coloured circle.

*Tip:* when you have aligned objects, it can be helpful to use **Manipulate/Group** (keyboard shortcut CTRL+G) to convert the aligned block into a permanent group.

# Flipping an object

You can flip an object automatically to make a vertical or horizontal mirror image of it. For example, symbol 13230 is a finger pointing to the right. To make a finger which points to the left, use **Draw/Symbol...** to place symbol 13230 on the page and then choose **Manipulate/Flip/Horizontally** to make the finger point to the left.

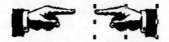

In a similar way, **Manipulate/Flip/Vertically** makes a vertical mirror image of an object.

## Stacking

You can use **Manipulate/Stacking Order** to alter objects' positions in a heap of objects. Generally speaking, the most recently placed object will be at the 'front' and will obscure anything which is 'behind' it. In the example below, there are two objects, a maple leaf and a rectangle with a graduated fill. The maple leaf was drawn first and so it is hidden behind the rectangle.

*(Left) The rectangle is on top of the maple leaf (Right) Stacking order reversed. The maple leaf is on top*

To reverse the order, select the rectangle and choose **Manipulate/Stacking Order/Send to Back**. (Or use the keyboard shortcut CTRL+K.) This will put the rectangle behind the maple leaf as a background.

Equally, you could select the maple leaf and choose **Manipulate/Stacking Order/Bring to Front** (or

55

use the keyboard shortcut CTRL+F) to achieve the same result.

## Making Objects Proportional

If an object has had its aspect ratio distorted, for example by dragging on its edge handles, it can easily be restored to its original aspect ratio by selecting the distorted image and then choosing **Manipulate/Make Proportional.**

*This little piggy is distorted, but using Make Proportional he's back to normal*

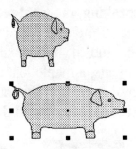

# 5. Symbols and Custom Libraries

## Overview of Symbols

*Apprentice* has a wide range of Symbols. The program is different to most other drawing packages in that the number of Symbols included is very large at over 3000. *Apprentice* Symbols fall into three categories: *Shapes*, *Pictograms*, and *Icons*.

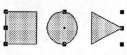 ■ ***Shapes***, obviously, are things like circles, squares, stars and geometric shapes.

 ***Pictograms*** are miniature pictures of real items, varying from jet aircraft to vegetables.

 ***Icons*** are stylised representations of people, things or activities. Icons are often used on the signs found in public places. *Apprentice*'s icons include a full range of 'stick people' from sportsmen through to police officers.

Full details of the *Apprentice* Symbols can be found in the *Arts & Letters Clip Art Handbook*. There are also more complicated, full-colour pieces of Clip-art, things like maps, cartoons, animals, landmarks and so on. Each item of Clip-art is made up of several Symbols, and in some cases freeform objects drawn with the *Arts &Letters Editor*. Again,

57

full details can be found in the *Arts & Letters Clip Art Handbook.*

## Drawing a Symbol

In order to draw a symbol, you must first access the Symbol dialog. To do this, you can either click the mouse pointer on the Symbol Tool, choose

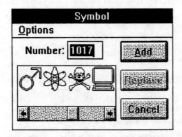

**Draw/Symbol...** or use the keyboard shortcut CTRL+S. This will display the Symbol dialog on the screen.

Choose a Symbol to add either by clicking on one of the Symbols included in the limited selection displayed in the dialog above the scroll bar (you can scroll left and right to reveal more symbols; although the number of symbols included in the selection is quite small, the major geometric symbols such as squares, circles stars and triangles are here), or by typing the symbol's reference number from the *Arts & Letters Clip Art Handbook* in the Number box and clicking on the Add button. The mouse pointer will change to the Add Item tool. To actually place the symbol in your document, click the left mouse button once to place the object at its default size. Alternatively, to place the Symbol at a size of your choosing, click and drag the mouse pointer. As you drag, you will see an outline appearing. When the outline appears as big as you want the Symbol to be, release the mouse button and the Symbol will flow into the space.

If you have deleted the file containing the Symbol

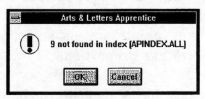

whose reference number you have entered, or entered an invalid reference number, an error message will be displayed.

By default, the Symbol's aspect ratio is preserved. If you wish to distort the aspect ratio, hold down the CTRL key during dragging. *This is the opposite of many other Windows applications.*

When a Symbol is the selected object, its reference number appears in the Status Bar.

If a Symbol on screen is already selected when the Add Symbol dialog is opened, the Replace button will be ungreyed, and in this case clicking on the Replace button instead of the Add button will replace the original Symbol with the newly chosen one.

# Resizing Symbols and modifying their aspect ratios

In order to resize a symbol, it must first be selected by clicking on it with the mouse pointer so that handles - small black squares - appear at each corner and at the midpoint of each edge. Drag on a corner handle to resize the symbol maintaining its aspect ratio. Drag on a edge handle to make the symbol wider, narrower, taller or shorter. To restore a symbol to its 'proper' size and aspect ratio, choose **Manipulate/Make Proportional**.

Like any other objects, Symbols can be slanted, rotated, coloured, and filled. Additionally they can be converted into freeform objects.

# Using Custom Libraries

Custom Symbols are *Apprentice*'s clip art symbols, precoloured graphics of a more complicated nature, for example animals, vehicles, maps and landmarks. They are of a high quality, and provide an excellent basis for including in your own designs. They are stored in Custom Libraries which are managed with the Clip-art Manager.

# Drawing a Custom Symbol

In order to draw a Custom Symbol (piece of
Clip-Art), start the Clip-Art Manager by clicking on

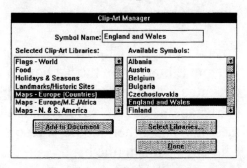

the Library Tool, choosing **Draw/Clip-Art
Manager** or pressing CTRL+C.

This brings up the Clip-Art Manager. In the list box
on the left, the names of the available Custom
Libraries are shown. The names of the individual
Custom Symbols from the selected library appear in
the list box on the right.

*The Hot Air Balloon
from the
Transportation
library*

To add a Custom Library to the list of available
libraries, click on the Select Libraries... button and

double click on its name in the list box. Custom Libraries have the extension .YAL.

The *Apprentice* Clip Art libraries are quite extensive and more pieces can be ordered from Computer Support Corporation.

To add a piece of Clip-Art to a document, select a Custom Library from the list box on the left by clicking on its name (double-clicking on one of the entries in this list box displays an informational message) and either double-click on the piece of Clip-Art's name in the list box on the right, or select its name in the list box and click on the Add to Document button.

The mouse pointer will change to the Add Item tool. To actually place the piece of Clip-Art in your document, click the left mouse button once (or press the spacebar) to place the picture at its default size. Alternatively, to place it at a size of your choosing, click and drag the mouse pointer. As you drag, you will see an outline appearing. When the outline appears as big as you want the piece of Clip-Art to be, release the mouse button.

By default, the Clip-Art's aspect ratio is preserved. If you wish to distort the aspect ratio, hold down the CTRL key during dragging. *This is the opposite of many other Windows programs.*

# Modifying a Custom Symbol

Custom Symbols consist of several objects, which are either *Apprentice* Symbols or freeform objects drawn with the *Arts & Letters Graphics Editor.* In

*The map of The Netherlands includes a national flag*

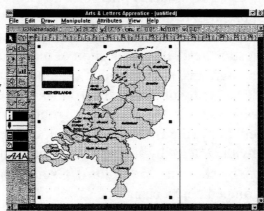

*.... which can itself be split into its four constituent parts*

addition to manipulating the piece of Clip-Art as one object, you can break the Custom Symbol up into its constituent parts and manipulate each part individually. For example, the map of The

Netherlands consists of the country outline, the provincial borders, the labels and the flag, all of which can be further broken down into their constituent parts.

Once you've broken a piece of Clip Art apart, it's important to realise that it's no longer a group which can be moved, rotated, slanted or resized as a single object; instead, it's a collection of individual objects or sub-groups, each of which can only be moved independently of the others. To make the collection of objects back into a cohesive group it's necessary to either use the Block Select Tool, or select individual items by shift-clicking and then grouping them by choosing **Manipulate/Group**. The regrouped object cannot be saved as a new Custom Symbol using *Apprentice*, but can be saved in a GED file.

## Converting Symbols to Freeform Objects

Symbols are all solid objects, and converting a solid object to a freeform object is easy. Select the object which you wish to convert by clicking on it with the Pointer Tool, and choose **Draw/Cvt to Freeform** (or use the keyboard shortcut F8). While the conversion is going on, the pointer will change to the hourglass, as the conversion process may take some time especially if a complex object is selected. When the object has been converted, the message in the status bar will change to Closed Shape if the

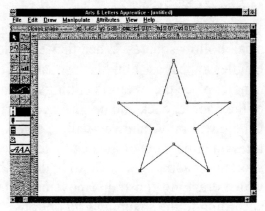

Symbol was made up of a single object (e.g. the
five-pointed star, Symbol # 1651) or Block (*xx*
objects) if the symbol is more complicated (e.g. the
credit cards icon, Symbol # 5165, which is made up
of five objects).

## Freeform editing a closed shape

To edit a closed shape, first of all select the shape
which you wish to edit by clicking on it with the
pointer tool. Enter freeform editing mode by
selecting the Freeform Tool from the toolbox or by
choosing **Draw/Edit Freeform** (keyboard shortcut
CTRL+P). In freeform editing mode, several options
in the Draw and View menus are ungreyed.

Once you have entered freeform editing mode, the
selected solid shape appears without a fill as a series
of sections (lines or curves) with a handle at the join
between two sections.

## Moving handles

When they are not selected, point handles appear as small hollow squares. When they are selected, handles appear as solid black squares. To move a handle, place the freeform editing tool in the centre of the handle, click and drag. As you drag, the handle will move and you will be able to see the lines on either side of the handle lengthening, shortening and moving. Holding down the SHIFT key whilst dragging constrains movement of the handle according to the snapping grid options.

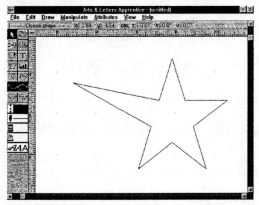

You can also move handles with the keyboard. It's often easier to make fine adjustments with the keyboard rather than the mouse. To move a handle with the keyboard, position the freeform editing tool over the handle's centre (try using the Zoom tool to enlarge the area you are working on if this is difficult) but do *not* hold down the mouse button. Hold down the spacebar and move the handle to the left or right, or up or down by pressing one of the arrow keys. When you have finished moving the handle, release the spacebar.

## Adding handles

Whilst in freeform editing mode, press F5 to turn
the freeform editing tool into the handle adding
tool. Add the handle either using the mouse by
placing the handle adding tool's arrow at the desired
point on the outline and clicking the mouse button
or position it at the desired point on the line with
the arrow keys and pressing the spacebar.

## Deleting handles

To delete a handle, either select it by clicking on it
with the freeform editing tool and press the delete
key; or select it by positioning the freeform editing
tool over it and pressing the spacebar and then
delete it by pressing the delete key.

## Viewing and moving control points

Control points control the shape of a Bézier curve
associated with a handle. Handles on straight lines
do not have control points. To view a handle's

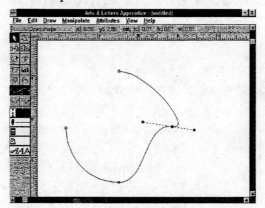

control points, first select the handle and then

choose **View/Control Points** or use the keyboard shortcut CTRL+4.

Control points appear as two black squares connected to the handle with a dashed line. Moving the control points alters the appearance of the curve without moving the handle. To move a control point, either drag it with the mouse or by positioning the freeform editing tool over the control point, holding down the spacebar and using the arrow keys to navigate.

### Leaving freeform editing mode

To leave freeform editing mode, either click the right mouse button once, choose **Draw/Edit freeform** or use the keyboard shortcut CTRL+P. When you leave freeform editing mode, the object will be redrawn complete with its fill pattern and will appear with the normal handles around it.

## Shadow effects with Symbols and Custom Symbols

### Symbols

Shadow effects are a good way of enhancing your

designs and *Apprentice* makes it easy to create them. As an example, we'll show how a variety of different effects can be applied to one basic symbol. The symbol we'll use is #3111, the businessman wearing a hat.

The first thing to do is to make a duplicate of our businessman using the Duplicate Tool. The duplicate is needed so that effects can be applied to the original.

The first shadow effect is the simplest. It throws a shadow directly behind the figure as if spotlighted against a wall. The figure at the front (the duplicate) has been coloured black; the 'shadow' at the back is filled with a light dither, and enlarged by 20% or so. The symbols have then been aligned so that they are in line vertically and in line at the bottom.

For a slightly more complex shadow, as produced by the evening sun, the rear symbol has been slanted and the two symbols left aligned.

You can even make the businessman have a shadow that isn't his, by using the Symbol dialog's Replace function to replace the rear symbol with a different one. In this case, we've used the Guardsman, # 3944.

The same principle applies to creating shadow effects with any Symbol

Experiment with different ideas, including applying different colours and fills, using multiple shadows, using different alignments, slants and rotations.

## Custom Symbols

The same general ideas apply. For example, here is the Leaning Tower of Pisa with its own shadow:

Or you could get silly and make it cast Big Ben's shadow:

Other pieces of Clip-Art, for example the maps, which include several distinct parts, may need to be broken down into their constituent parts before you can apply a shadow effect.

As with all *Apprentice* effects, the only way to find out what does and doesn't work is to experiment.

# 6. Text

## Adding Text to a design

Although you may simply use *Apprentice* to draw
graphics to add to documents created with other
programs, it is an ideal program for creating posters,
menus and similar small documents which contain a
mixture of text and graphics. Because *Apprentice*
treats both text and graphics in a similar way, you
can easily add fill styles and patterns to type to
create one-off text effects to import into other
programs.

## Text strings

Text strings are words, groups of words, and
individual alphanumeric characters entered via the
Text Entry dialog, or imported with **File/Import.....**

## Freeform text

Freeform text is a text string which has been
converted to freeform objects by using **Draw/Cvt to
Freeform**. Once text has been converted to into
freeform objects, it cannot be converted back to
text. *Apprentice* treats freeform text just like any
other freeform object. This means that outlines can
be modified using the freeform editing tools to
make unique lettering styles.

# Typefaces

## Apprentice typefaces or printer typefaces?
This is a decision which should not arise too often as most of the popular commercial fonts have differently named equivalents in the *Apprentice* typeface set. (See Appendix E for a list.)

Sometimes, you may wish to create an effect using a fancy typeface from your collection of TrueType or ATM (PostScript) fonts. *Apprentice* will let you use both TrueType (Windows 3.1) and Adobe Type Manager (ATM) fonts in your designs. It regards them as Printer Fonts. However, *Apprentice* handles Printer Fonts differently to its own. You cannot apply a fill style to a text string in a non-*Apprentice* font, but you can alter its colour using the Line Color function. You cannot convert text strings in TrueType fonts, Windows bitmap fonts or printer resident fonts to freeform text (objects). A piece of text in a PostScript font can be converted to a collection of freeform objects, and those freeform objects can then have a fill style applied to them. You cannot convert *Apprentice* typefaces into other formats.

To use printer fonts rather than *Apprentice* fonts, select the printer name radio button in the Type Attributes dialog; note that you can't use a mixture of Apprentice and printer fonts in the same document, you must choose one or the other. You

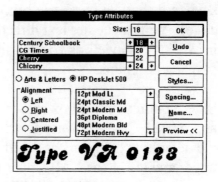

must have selected a printer using **File/Printer Setup...** before you can use printer fonts.

Because *Apprentice* looks for font files used with text strings on your PC's hard disk, if you create a design which includes a text string in a particular font and save it as a GED file, and then transfer that GED file to another PC running *Apprentice*, which you may want to do to print out via a different printer, then that PC must also have that font available. To avoid this possible problem, convert text strings to freeform objects if you wish to make the GED file 'portable'.

## Adding text to a design

To add text to a design, either choose the Text Tool from the Toolbox, choose **Draw/Text...** or use the

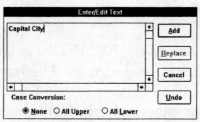

keyboard shortcut CTRL+T to bring up the text entry dialog. You can't enter text directly on to the screen in WYSIWYG view as you can in some other drawing programs.

Enter your text in the box and choose the appropriate Case Conversion radio button: None is the default; text appears as typed in a mixture of upper and lower case; All Upper forces all the text to upper case (CAPITALS); All Lower forces all the text to lower case (small letters). Next, click on the Add button. The mouse pointer changes to the Add Object tool; click the left mouse button once to add the text string at the default size and style, or click and drag the tool to create a dashed outline 'box' for the text to flow into when you release the mouse button. Note that text entered in the text entry dialog does not automatically wrap around. If you wish to start a new line, press the return key.

Note that **all** text in the same dialog will be part of the same text string and will have the same typeface and other attributes. You cannot have half of a text string in one typeface and the other half in another typeface. If you require this effect you will have to place the text in two separate strings and align them by moving them around and using **Manipulate/Align...**.

Alternatively, if you have a larger amount of text to place into a design, use **File/Import...** to bring up the Import dialog, choose Text Only as the filter and then either highlight the desired filename and click on the OK button or double-click on the desired filename. The mouse pointer changes to the Add Object tool; click the left mouse button once to add the imported text string at the default size and style,

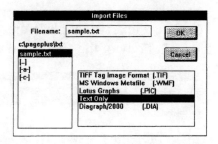

or click and drag the tool to create a dashed outline 'box' for the text to flow into when you release the mouse button.

Text imported like this should not contain control codes inserted by word processors as *Apprentice* cannot strip them out.

## Editing text strings

You can't edit text in WYSIWYG view in *Apprentice*. You must use the Edit/Enter text dialog. To edit a piece of text, first select it. Then either dlick on the Text Tool or choose **Draw/Text....** The Edit/Enter Text dialog will appear, displaying the selected text highlighted, that is as white on black. Make your changes and click on the Replace button to subsitute the changed text for the original text. If you click on the New button at this stage you will add another text string containing the amended wording to the design.

## Moving a text string

To move a text string, place the mouse pointer over the main body of the text (*not* the handles). Press

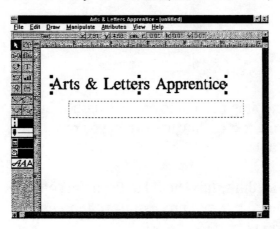

and hold down the left mouse button to 'pick up' the text. A dashed outline representing the text's bounding box appears. Drag the mouse pointer, releasing the left mouse button when the dashed outline is over the text's desired new position. The text will then be displayed properly again.

### Moving text using the keyboard

To move text exactly horizontally or vertically, select it as normal by clicking on it. Place the mouse pointer on the main part of the text, but do not hold the mouse button down. Press and hold down the spacebar. A dashed outline representing the text's bounding box appears. Still holding down the spacebar, move the text up with the Up arrow, left with the Left arrow, right with the Right arrow or down with the Down arrow. When you have finished moving the text, release the spacebar.

## DuplicatingText

The quickest way of copying text is to use the Duplicate Tool. Firstly, choose the Duplicate Tool from the Toolbox. The mouse pointer changes to the Duplicate Tool. Click and drag on the text which

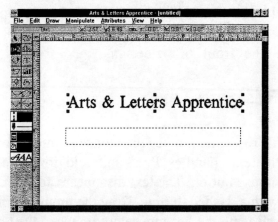

you wish to copy. You will see a dashed outline being dragged. This outline represents the copy of the text. When you release the mouse button, the copy will be displayed properly. Duplicating text like this is not like using the **Edit/Copy** and **Edit/Paste** commands which are standard Windows functions using the Clipboard. The Duplicate function does not make use of the Clipboard at all, and is therefore faster.

## Duplicating text using the keyboard

To copy text and place the copy using the keyboard, place the Duplicate Tool on the main part of the text, but do not hold the mouse button down. Press and hold down the spacebar. A dashed outline appears representing the copy of the text. Still holding down the spacebar, move the outline up with the Up arrow, left with the Left arrow, right with the Right arrow or down with the Down arrow. When you have finished moving the outline, release the spacebar to display the copied text properly. **Note:** text copied using the Duplicate Tool is placed at the 'front' of the design.

# Resizing Text

To resize text, place the mouse pointer over one of the text's handles. Press and hold down the left mouse button. The text disappears and is replaced with a dashed outline. Drag the mouse pointer, releasing the left mouse button when the text's dashed outline is the same as the desired new size. The text will then be displayed at its new size. Dragging on a corner handle will resize the text proportionally. Dragging on an edge handle will resize the text without keeping it in proportion, giving the impression of expansion or compression. The changes which you make by resizing will be reflected in the Type Attributes dialog - for

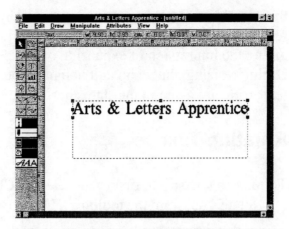

example, you might have resized the text to be 62.7 points in size or extended it to be 115% of its normal width. Do not try to make precise sizing adjustments by dragging; always enter new values in the Text Attributes dialog.

## Resizing text using the keyboard

You may find it easier to make fine movements with the keyboard controls rather than the mouse. To resize text using the keyboard, select it as normal by clicking on it. Place the mouse pointer on one of the text's handles, but do not hold the mouse button down. Press and hold down the spacebar. A dashed outline appears as well as the text. Still holding down the spacebar, resize the outline using the arrow keys. When you have finished resizing the outline, release the spacebar to draw in the text at its new size. Placing the cursor on a corner handle, holding down the spacebar and holding down an arrow key will resize the text proportionally. Placing the cursor on an edge handle, holding down the spacebar and holding down an arrow key will resize the text without keeping it in proportion, giving the impression of expansion or compression. During resizing, the width and height of the selected text string are given in the status bar.

## Rotating Text

To rotate a text string, first of all select it. Choose the Rotate Tool from the toolbox. The mouse

pointer changes to a small arrow with a rotation symbol. The centre of rotation appears as a cross hair on a circle at the centre of the text. It can be moved by dragging it with the Rotate Tool. Rotate the text by dragging on one of its corner handles with the rotate tool. A dashed outline, representing the new position of the text's bounding box, will be seen moving as you drag. The amount of rotation (in degrees) is shown in the Status Bar after the r:.

Clicking the right mouse button leaves rotation mode.

## Rotating text using the keyboard

You may find it easier to make fine movements with the keyboard controls rather than the mouse. To rotate text with greater control over the degree of rotation, select it as normal by clicking on it. Choose the Rotate Tool and place the tool's pointer on one of the corner handles, but do not hold the mouse button down. Press and hold down the spacebar. A dashed outline appears around the text. Still holding down the spacebar, rotate the text anticlockwise with the Up or Left arrow keys, or clockwise with the Right or Down arrow keys. The amount of rotation (in degrees) is shown in the Status Bar after the r:. When you have finished rotating the text, release the spacebar.

# Slanting Text

To slant a piece of text, first of all select it. Choose the Slant Tool from the toolbox. The mouse pointer changes to a small arrow with the slant symbol. The centre of slant appears as a cross hair on a circle at the centre of the text. It can be moved by dragging it with the Slant Tool. Slant the text by dragging on one of its handles with the slant tool. A dashed outline, representing the new position of the text's bounding box, will move as you drag. The amount of slant (in degrees) is shown in the Status Bar after the h: and v:. Release the mouse button to redraw the slanted text. Clicking the right mouse button leaves slant mode.

## Slanting text using the keyboard

You may find it easier to make fine movements with the keyboard controls rather than the mouse. To slant text with greater control over the degree of slant, select it as normal by clicking on it. Choose the Slant Tool and place the tool's pointer on one of the corner handles, but do not hold the mouse button down. Press and hold down the spacebar. A dashed outline appears around the text. Still holding down the spacebar, slant the text vertically with the Up or Down arrow keys, or horizontally with the Right or Left arrow keys. The amount of vertical and/or horizontal slant (in degrees) is shown in the Status Bar after the h: and v:. When you have finished slanting the text, release the spacebar to redraw the slanted text.

# Setting Type Attributes

Type attributes are a combination of the following:
- Typeface and Style (font);
- Size;
- Alignment;
- Letter space, Word space, Leading and Kerning;
- Type width.

**Attributes/Type...** (keyboard shortcut CTRL+Y) brings up the Type Attributes dialog where you can set these options with great precision.
The Type Attributes dialog has these elements:

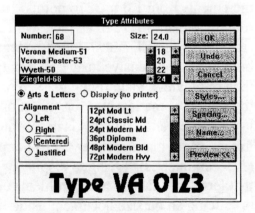

- a box displaying the *Apprentice* reference number of the selected typeface;
- a box displaying the size (in points) chosen;

- a list box with the names of available fonts;
- a list box with pre-set sizes;
- a box with alignment radio buttons;
- a list box of named text styles;
- OK, Undo and Cancel buttons;
- Styles..., Spacing..., and Names... buttons which lead to further dialogs;
- a Preview button which turns on or off a preview of the selected font.

## Size

Enter the desired text size in the Size box, or select one of the pre-set sizes from the pre-set sizes list box. You can specify any size, in 0.1 point increments from 1.0 to 3276 points. 1.0 point is roughly equal to 1/72 of an inch, which is ridiculously small, and wouldn't be legible on all but the most expensive imagesetter output and even then only with a magnifying glass. 5 or 6 points is the smallest practical size for output on a standard laser printer, and 10 points is nearer the mark on an ink jet or dot matrix printer. 3276 points is 45.5" (115 centimetres). Trying to display or print type that large will cause severe problems unless you are producing an outsize document using tiled printing. Usually, type sizes between 10 and 350 points will be sufficient. Text of 800 point size will almost completely fill an A4 page in portrait orientation. If you need a precise type size, always enter it in the Type Attributes dialog rather than trying to fit it by eye.

## Typeface

Select a typeface from the list box. This will show either *Arts & Letters* fonts or printer fonts. If the Preview option has been turned on by clicking on the Preview >> button, a preview of the selected typeface is displayed in an extension to the dialog box. (If the Preview function is already on, clicking on the Preview << button will turn it off.)

## Alignment

If you have got more than one line of text, you may wish to use the Text Alignment radio buttons to align the lines relative to one another. Left aligns lines to be flush against the left of the text block (ragged right), Right aligns the lines to be flush against the right edge of the text block (ragged left), Centre aligns the items to the text block's centre line and Justify pushes the text out so that it is flush against both the left and right edges of the text block. The default alignment is Left.

## Named Styles

You can select a named attribute from the list box to the right of the list of available fonts. Named attributes are pre-set combinations of typeface and style, sizes and spacing.

## Type Styles

Clicking on the Styles button brings up the Type Styles dialog. This allows you to choose whether a typeface should be Normal, **Bold**, *Italic*, ~~Strikeout~~, <u>Underlined</u> or a ***<u>combination</u>*** of styles. If a style is

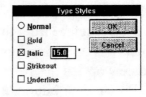

not available for use with a particular typeface, it is grayed out. Choose a style by checking a check box. If *italic* style is available and chosen, you will be able to specify the angle at which the letters should slope. The default angle is 15.0°.

## Type Spacing

Clicking on the Spacing button brings up the Type Spacing Adjustment dialog, where you can specify spacing options.

*The check boxes and value boxes in the Type Spacing Adjustment dialog allow you to set spacing options*

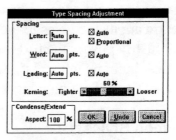

**Letter space** is the space between letters, expressed in points. If the Auto check box is checked, *Apprentice* will work out the value automatically. If the box is unchecked, you can enter a value manually in the Letter points box. The default is Auto. You can also choose whether to make the letter spacing proportional (that is, varying according to the width of the letter) or not by

checking or unchecking the Proportional check box.
The default is Proportional.

**Word space** is the space between words, expressed
in points. If the Auto box is checked (the default),
Apprentice works out the value automatically. You
can uncheck the Auto box and enter a value
manually in the Word points box.

**Leading** is the space between lines of text. If the
Auto box is checked (the default) Apprentice will
work out the leading value automatically. You can
uncheck the Auto box and enter a value manually in
the Leading points box.

**Kerning** affects the spacing between pairs of letters
and is expressed as a percentage. It can be made
tighter or looser using the scroll bar. Kerning cannot
be applied if Proportional spacing is turned off. If
Proportional spacing is turned off, the Kerning
scroll bar is grayed out.

**Condense/Extend.** Letters can be extended (made
wider) or condensed (made narrower) by entering a
value in the Condense/Extend box. You can enter
any value between 1% and 6398%; however at
extreme values the letters may not display correctly.
Mostly, values between 50% and 250% will be
appropriate. The default value is 100% (of normal
width).

Classic Medium 50%
Classic Medium 75%
Classic Medium 100%
Classic Medium 125%
Classic Medium 150%

It's worth noting that if the *Apprentice* default is Auto, it will produce a result which is usually acceptable. Setting the values manually will mean considerable extra effort, and will often produce only a minor improvement which probably won't be noticed, and so it's sensible to use the Auto default if only to save work.

## Naming Styles

Clicking on the Name... button brings up the Name Attributes dialog. Using this dialog, you can assign a name to a particular typeface/size/spacing style

which you have created; that name will then appear in the predefined styles list box. You can also rename an existing style. The name can be as descriptive as you like; it's not like a filename which has to comply with DOS rules.

When you have finished changing the type attributes, click on OK to accept the changes, Cancel to abandon the changes and close the Type Attributes dialog, or Undo to abandon the changes but keep the Type Attributes dialog open.

The changes made with the Type Attributes dialog, apply to the text selected when the dialog was opened, and to all text entered or imported after closing the dialog until further changes are made.

## Converting Text Strings to Freeform Text

Converting a text string to a series of freeform objects is easy. Select the text string which you whish to convert by clicking on it with the Pointer Tool, and choose **Draw/Cvt to Freeform** (or use the keyboard shortcut F8). The pointer will change to the hourglass, as the conversion process may take some time especially if a large text string is selected. When all the text has been converted, the message in the status bar will change to Block (*xx* objects).

There will almost certainly be more objects in the Block than there were letters in the text string. This is because, when converted to freeform objects, letters like *g* and *d* are made up of more than one shape. The *g* for example is made up of the main part and two white eyes in the body. You can break the block apart by clicking on one of its elements

*The letter g is made up of three objects: body and two eyes*

with the pointer tool. Once text has been converted

to a series of freeform objects, remember that each part of a letter is now simply a freeform shape which is independent of all other objects on the page.

Once text has been converted to freeform objects, its constituent parts can be edited and manipulated like any other freeform object.

Text which has been converted to a series of freeform objects cannot be reassembled into a typeface.

## Suggestions for effects using text converted to freeform objects

These are just a few ideas to get you started. The possibilities are virtually endless.

**Delete 'eyes' from individual letters**

**Rem●ve
the eyes**

**Replace the 'eyes' with symbols**

**Rotate individual components of a letter, word or sentence**

**Rotate Individual letters**

or words

**Resize individual letters**

BIGGER SMALLER

**Edit the outlines of individual letters**

**Stretch bars, arms, ascenders or descenders**

**Add nodes and make outlines more complex**

**Remove nodes and make outlines simpler**

## Shadow Effects

### Drop Shadows

To create a drop shadow effect, make a copy of the text which you wish to apply a shadow effect to, using the Copy Tool. Make the copy go 'behind' the original by using **Manipulate/Stacking Order/Send to back**. Apply a different fill style and colouring to the text which forms the shadow.

**Shadow**

### Enhanced Shadows

Enhance your shadow effects by distorting or manipulating the shadow. Here are just two ideas which you may like to try.

# Shadow

# Shadow

It cannot be stressed strongly enough that these are just a couple of very simple ideas. You can create literally thousands of variations if you are prepared to spend the time. The only way to find out whether or not something works is to *try it for yourself.*

## Reverse Outs

Reverse Outs, sometimes known as WOBs (White on Black) are a simple yet effective attention grabber, often used in posters or newspaper headlines.

To create this effect in *Apprentice*, simply create a background of the appropriate size, usually by adding the square symbol from the Symbol dialog and resizing it so that it forms a rectangle. Give it the appropriate fill and line attributes, such as solid black. Then, add the text and colour it white. Use **Manipulate/Align Items** to put the text neatly on the background.

Finally, it's a good idea to put the effect into a permanent group using **Manipulate/Group** so that you don't accidentally break it apart when moving it to its final position in the design.

## Mirror effects

Mirror effects can easily be created by using the Duplicate tool and then using **Manipulate/Flip** on

the duplicate text string. Use **Manipulate/Align**

**Items...** to line the effect up properly. It's a good idea to put the effect into a permanent group using **Manipulate/Group** so that you don't accidentally break it apart when moving it to its final position in the design.

# 7. Working with Lines and Curves

## Overview

Lines and curves are the basic elements of freeform objects. They can be used to create open or closed shapes, and a symbol which has been converted to a freeform object is made up of a number of lines and curves.

## Drawing Lines

Using lines and curves, you can build up your own freeform objects if you wish to and draw lines and curves to bind text to, although most of the time it's possible (and far easier) to simply modify Symbols or other objects. *Apprentice*'s line drawing tools are located in the toolbox on the left of the screen, below the general tools but above the attribute tools.

### Straight Lines
To draw a straight line click on the line drawing tool icon in the toolbox, or choose **Draw/Line** (keyboard shortcut F2) to change the mouse pointer into the Line Drawing Tool. Position the Line Drawing Tool on the page where you want the line's starting point to be, click the left mouse button and drag the Line Drawing Tool to where you want the line's end point to be. You will see a thin black line

being drawn between the line's starting point and

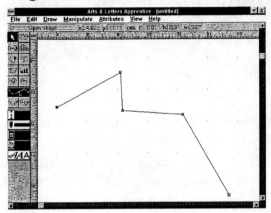

the position of the Line Drawing Tool. Release the
mouse button to finish drawing. Handles appear at
both ends of the line. You can move these handles
with the freeform editing tool. To change the line
drawing tool for the freeform editing tool, click the
right mouse button once. Click the right mouse
button twice or use the keyboard shortcut CTRL+P to
leave line drawing mode.

In line drawing mode, all lines are shown as single
thin black lines. To see them as they will actually
appear, leave line drawing mode by clicking the
right mouse button twice or using CTRL+P. A
preview of the line attributes is displayed as a
reminder in the line attributes tool.

## Curves
To draw a curve, click on the curve drawing tool
icon in the toolbox, or choose **Draw/Curve**
(keyboard shortcut F3) to change the mouse pointer

into the Curve Drawing Tool. Position the Curve
Drawing Tool on the page where you want the
curve's starting point to be, click the left mouse
button and drag the Curve Drawing Tool to where
you want the curve's end point to be. Try to draw as
smooth a line as possible as this will affect the
number of Bézier segments in the curve, depending
on how you have set the Snap Options. You will see

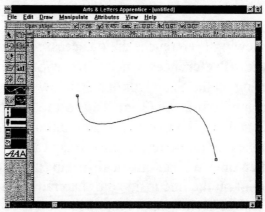

a thin black line being drawn between the starting
point and the position of the Curve Drawing Tool.
Release the mouse button to finish drawing. The
hourglass appears while *Apprentice* calculates the
number of Bézier segments in the curve. Point
Handles appear at the ends of each Bézier segment.
You can move these points with the freeform
editing tool. To change the curve drawing tool for
the freeform editing tool, click the right mouse
button once. Click the right mouse button twice to
leave curve drawing mode.

In curve drawing mode and freeform editing mode,
all lines are shown as single thin black lines. To see

them as they will actually appear, leave curve drawing mode by clicking the right mouse button twice or using CTRL+P. A preview of the line attributes is displayed as a reminder in the line attributes tool.

## Setting Snap Options

Choose **Draw/Snap To** to access a submenu with the choice of snapping to the Grid or snapping to points. The snapping grid is set up from the Viewing Preferences dialog accessed with **View/Preferences**. Choose **Draw/Snap Options** to bring up the Snap Options dialog which controls the snapping if **Draw/Snap To** is set to Points.

This dialog contains two radio buttons and two boxes for numeric values. If Snap to First is chosen, then lines will automatically snap (jump to) the first point on the line inside the snap radius. If Snap to Nearest is chosen, the line will snap to the nearest

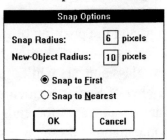

point inside the snap radius. Snap Radius controls the radius (in pixels) around a point from within which a line will snap to a point. This is not an easy concept to explain, but the effect of setting this to a higher value is to increase the amount of smoothing which *Apprentice* carries out. When drawing a

100

curve, *Apprentice* starts a new Bézier segment whenever the line drawn with the mouse wanders more than the set number of pixels: freehand drawing with a mouse is notoriously difficult, and a value of around 25-30 pixels is probably best for general use. [On a system using a VGA monitor at 640 x 480 pixels that is; on a SVGA display at a higher resolution (more pixels per inch) you may need to increase the value. Experiment!] The New Object Radius sets the distance from the end of a curve or line within which new curves or lines will be automatically joined to the existing line or curve.

You can change the snapping options at any time; for example you could start off with Snap To Grid chosen and later change to Snap To Points.

## Freeform editing a line or curve

To freeform edit a line or curve, first of all select the line or curve which you wish to edit by clicking on it with the pointer tool. Enter freeform editing mode by selecting the Freeform Tool from the toolbox or by choosing **Draw/Edit Freeform** (keyboard shortcut CTRL+P). In freeform editing mode, several options in the Draw and View menus are ungreyed. Once you have entered freeform editing mode, a line appears without a fill as a thin black line; a curve appears as a series of Bézier sections with a point handle at the join between sections.

## Moving point handles

When they are not selected, point handles appear as small hollow squares. When they are selected, point handles appear as solid black squares. To move a point handle, place the freeform editing tool in the centre of the square, click and drag. As you drag, the point handle will move and you will be able to see the lines on either side of the point lengthening, shortening and moving. Holding down the shift key whilst dragging constrains movement of the point according to the snapping grid options. You can also move points with the keyboard. It's often easier to make fine adjustments with the keyboard rather than the mouse. To move a point with the keyboard, position the freeform editing tool over the point handle's centre (try using the Zoom tool to enlarge the area you are working on if this is difficult) but do *not* hold down the mouse button. Hold down the spacebar and move the handle by pressing one of the arrow keys. When you have finished moving the handle, release the spacebar.

## Adding handles

Whilst in freeform editing mode, press F5 to turn the freeform editing tool into the handle adding tool. Add the handle either using the mouse by placing the handle adding tool's arrow at the desired point on the line or curve and clicking the mouse button or using the keyboard position it at the desired point on the line or curve with the arrow keys and press the spacebar.

## Moving multiple point handles

To move several point handles, select all the point handles which you wish to move by using the mouse pointer and SHIFT+CLICK. Clicking and dragging on one of the selected handles will move all the selected point handles. Holding down the shift key whilst dragging constrains movement of the point according to the snapping grid options. You can also move multiple points with the keyboard in a similar way to moving a single point handle.

## Deleting point handles

To delete a point handle, either select it by clicking on it with the freeform editing tool and press the delete key; or select it by positioning the freeform editing tool over it and pressing the spacebar and then delete it by pressing the delete key.

## Deleting Multiple Point Handles

It is possible to delete several handles at once. To do this, select all the handles which you wish to delete either by using SHIFT-CLICK or the Block

*When multiple point handles are selected and the delete key is pressed, this mini-dialog appears*

Select Tool. When you have selected the handles which you wish to delete, press the delete key. This

will bring up a mini-dialog where you can choose to delete Points or Sections or cancel the operation. Choose Points to delete the selected point handles. Apprentice removes the handles and resmooths the curve.

## Deleting Sections

To delete a section, select the point handles at either end of it. Press the delete key. This will bring up a mini-dialog where you can choose to delete Points or Sections or cancel the operation. Choose

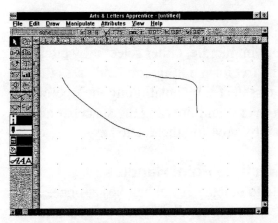

Sections to delete the section between the selected point handles. Apprentice removes the section, leaving two separate curves. If you have selected more than two handles, and choose to delete Sections, all the sections between the two endmost selected handles will be deleted.

## Viewing and moving control points

Control points control the shape of a Bézier curve associated with a handle. Handles on straight lines do not have control points. To view a handle's control points, first select the handle and then choose **View/Control Points** or use the keyboard

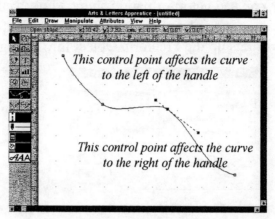

shortcut CTRL+4. Control points appear as two black squares connected to the handle with a dashed line. Moving the control points alters the appearance of the curve without moving the point handle. To move a control point, either drag it with the mouse or by positioning the freeform editing tool over the control point, holding down the spacebar and using the arrow keys to navigate.

## Leaving freeform editing mode
To leave freeform editing mode, either click the right mouse button once, choose **Draw/Edit freeform** or use the keyboard shortcut CTRL+P. When you leave freeform editing mode, the object will be redrawn complete with its fill pattern and will appear with the normal handles around it.

# Getting information about a line, open shape or curve

You can get information about a line, a curve or any open shape by choosing **Draw/Shape Info....** This brings up the Freeform Object Info dialog. The

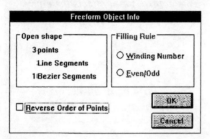

number of Points, Line Segments and Bézier Segments are displayed under the heading Open shape. The Filling Rule section is greyed out, as Fills cannot be applied to an open shape.

## Reversing the Point Order

Checking the Reverse Order of Points check box reverses the drawing order - for example, if you had

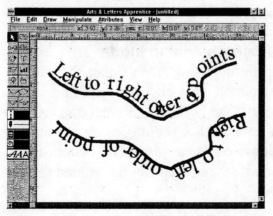

drawn a curve with six points and the first point on the left, checking this box would make the line's first point be the rightmost point. However the line's shape would be unaltered. This option is usually used in conjunction with text binding and is more useful in conjunction with closed shapes.

## Joining Lines and Curves

To join two lines and/or curves together to form one open shape, make sure that you are not in freeform editing mode, and then select both the lines and curves which you wish to join using the mouse pointer and SHIFT+CLICK.

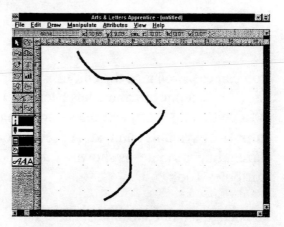

Choose **Draw/Join Open Shapes** or use the keyboard shortcut F7. The lines and/or curves which you have selected will then jump together automatically to form a single open shape. This function works on the idea that each line or curve end joins the nearest line or curve end. To a certain extent it is predictable, but it's a good idea to zoom

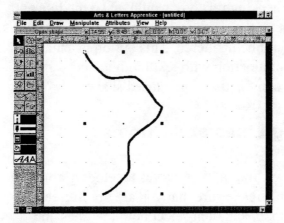

in on the objects you wish to join so you can see exactly what is likely to happen.

## Line Attributes

You can easily change the colour, style and width of lines. Once a line attrribute has been set, it remains in force for all subsequent lines, including the outlines of symbols and text. A preview of the current line attributes is shown in the Line Attributes Tool.

To change the line attributes, either click on the Line Attributes Tool or choose **Attributes/Line...** to bring up the Line Attributes dialog.

The Line Attributes dialog has four sections:

The Width section contains a value box where you can either enter a value for the line width or scroll up and down the available widths using the arrows. You can specify any value between 0 (hairline) and 72 points (1 inch) to 0.1 point precision. A preview of the line is shown below this box. The Scale width with object check box, if checked, makes *Apprentice* rescale the line if the object is resized.

The Pattern section contains five radio buttons for choosing the line pattern. The Auto-adjust check

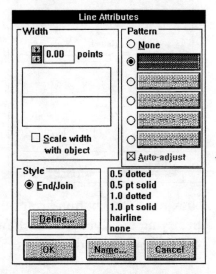

box adjusts the pattern to fit the lines shape and size.

The third section is a list of named styles. To use a named style, highlight its name in the list and click on OK. To create a new named style, adjust the Width and Pattern to your liking and click on the New button, then enter the new style's name in the mini-dialog and click on OK. This will make the new style appear in the list box.

109

A list of named styles can also be viewed by choosing **Attributes/Styles...** and then choosing **List/Lines**.

The fourth section contains a button marked Styles.

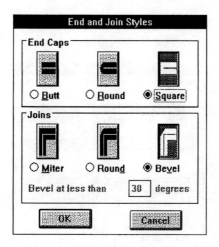

Clicking on this button brings up a dialog for specifying the style used to draw joins between sections and the ends of lines.

## Line Colour

To change the line colour, click on the Line Colour Tool or choose **Attributes/Color...** and pick a colour from the Named Color dialog. To apply the new colour attribute to fills as well as to the line, check the Fill check box as well as the Line check box. The line colour which you specify here will become the current line colour and will apply to all new lines and curves, including the outlines of symbols. The sample line in the Line Attributes Tool is displayed in either the current colour or the colour of the selected line, if it is different.

# 8. Colours and fills

## General

*Apprentice* supports the use of an almost infinite range of colours, both predefined and user defined. Colours can be used to enhance the appearance of your designs and can be applied as solid colours to lines and as different fill styles to closed shapes.

Of course, you won't be able to see the colours on your printed output unless you have access to a colour output device (e.g. colour printer or slide maker), but most Windows printer drivers for black and white printers do a reasonable job of converting what appears in colour on the screen to grey scales.

## Colour Palettes

Apprentice has many different named colour palettes, which have the extension pal and are stored in the `apprentc\palettes` subdirectory. A full-colour reference card is supplied with *Apprentice*, but sample Colour Palettes are also supplied in the Test Files section of the Activity Manager; printing them out is a good way of seeing how they will appear on output from your printer.

*Apprentice*'s default colour palette contains White, Black, Blue, Magenta, Cyan, Green, Yellow and Red. This can be seen in the Named Colors dialog. To bring up the Named Colors dialog, choose

**Attributes/Color...** or click on either the Line Colour Tool or the Fill Colour Tool.

The Named Colors dialog has its own menus.

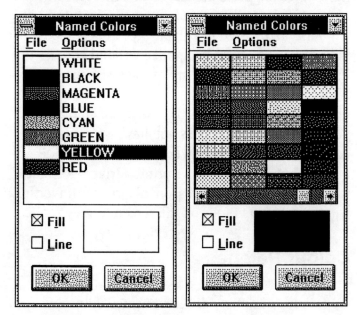

*The Named Colors dialog can be displayed either with or without the colour names being shown*

**File/New** clears the colours from the dialog. **File/Load/Save..** brings up a filing dialog for adding PAL colour palettes to the colours displayed. **Options/Mix** leads to a dialog for mixing your own colours. **Options/Show Names** toggles the display of colour names on and off. **Options/Stay** keeps the dialog permanently on display. If this option is selected the dialog will gain a border, system bar, minimize and maximize buttons. Our screen shots show the dialog set to stay on screen.

To add new colours to the existing selection, choose
**File/Load Save...** in the dialog to bring up the

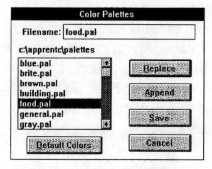

Color Palettes dialog. Select a PAL file from the
filing dialog, and click on the Append button to add
it to the existing range of colours. Clicking on the
Replace button replaces the existing colour
selection with the new palette (be careful not to
click on Replace when you actually mean Append),
and clicking on the Default Colors button resets the
current palette selection (after asking for

confirmation) to the default eight-colour palette.

It takes some time to build up a colour selection
containing several colour palettes; once you've built
up a custom colour selection you can save it under a
name of your choosing by choosing
**Options/Load/Save...**, typing a new name in the
Filename box and clicking on the Save button. Once

you have saved the custom palette, it can be recalled via the Named Color dialog's **Load/Save...** dialog like any other palette.

You can mix a custom colour by choosing **Options/Mix...** to bring up the Color Mixing dialog. Colour mixing can be carried out in one of three models: Hues, RGB (Red, Green, Blue) and CMYK (Cyan, Magenta, Yellow, Key). These

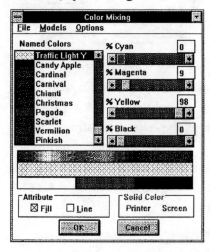

*Colour mixing can be carried out in one of three models: Hues, RGB or (as shown) CMYK.*

options are chosen from the Models menu. To alter the colour, use the horizontal scroll bars on the right of the dialog. Clicking on one of the named colours in the named colors list moves the scroll bars so as to indicate its proportions according to the model in use.

To name a colour which you have just mixed, choose **Options/Name...** to bring up a mini-dialog which you can also use to rename existing colours.

Colours can be applied to lines by clicking on the Line Colour Tool and to fills by clicking on the Fill Colour Tool. Changes are reflected in the colour of the line displayed in the Line Attributes Tool and the fill displayed in the Fill Attributes Tool. The current colour will be applied to all new objects.

## Fills

Colour fills can be applied to any closed shape, solid object or text string typed in an Apprentice typeface. Fills are applied via the Fill Attributes dialog. Choosing **Attributes/Fill**, using the keyboard shortcut CTRL+I, clicking on the Fill Attributes Tool or pressing the TAB key brings up the dialog. Using the dialog, you can choose the fill style to apply to the selected object(s).

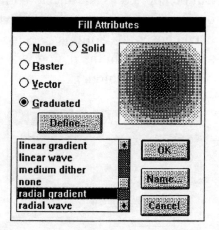

You can choose a named fill style from the list box at the bottom of the dialog or define a custom fill style using radio buttons and options.

There are five radio buttons, each of which selects a type of fill:

**Solid**. Solid fills are the simplest kind of fill which

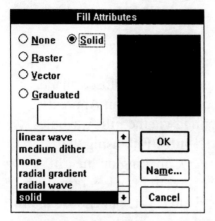

can be applied to an object. With a solid fill, the object is coloured solidly with whichever colour has been chosen. If Solid is selected as the fill type, the sample square in the dialog will be black (regardless of the chosen colour).

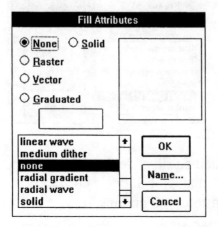

**None**. None as its name implies means that no fill pattern is applied to the object and it is transparent. If None is selected as the fill type, the sample square in the dialog will be blank.

**Raster**. Raster fills are fairly simple patterns which consist of various shading patterns, grids and so on.

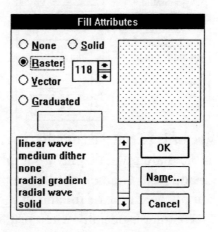

Each raster pattern has a reference number; enter this number in the raster number box, or scroll through the available patterns by clicking on the box's up and down arrows, and click on OK to select a raster pattern. If Raster is selected as the fill type, the sample square in the dialog will display a sample of the pattern. Note: do not use Raster shading patterns if you are sending output to a vector device like a plotter.

**Vector**. Vector fills are also known as dither patterns. To fill an object with a dither pattern, enter the pattern's reference number in the reference number box, or scroll through the available patterns by clicking on the box's up and down arrows, and click on OK to fill an object with a vector pattern. If

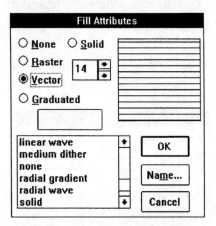

Vector is selected as the fill type, the sample square in the dialog will display a sample of the pattern. **Graduated**. Graduated fills are the most complicated type of fill and undoubtedly the most spectacular especially when printed in colour or viewed on screen. They should be used sparingly for two main reasons: firstly, they considerably slow down screen redraws, and secondly like any other

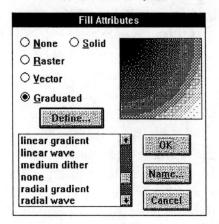

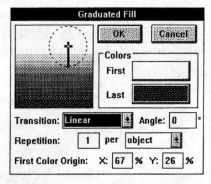

*Linear is the simplest type of graduated fill*

effect if they're overused they become clichéd and loose impact. If Graduated is selected as the fill type, the sample square in the dialog will display a sample of the current graduated fill. Clicking on the

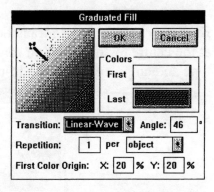

*Changes are shown in the dialog's preview box. This fill style is a Linear-Wave*

Define... button lets you further refine the definition of the graduated fill.

**Linear gradients** have a transition from one colour at the top to another at the bottom on a straight line basis. You can alter the transition type and angle, repetition and first colour origination point to create your own graduated fill style. The transition type and repetition style are altered from combo boxes; the transition angle and first colour origin can be

121

altered either by entering new values in the
appropriate boxes or by dragging the origination
point (to set the origin) or moving the angle
indicator.

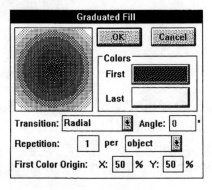

**Radial gradients** have a transition from one colour
at the centre to another. You can alter the transition
type and angle, repetition and first colour

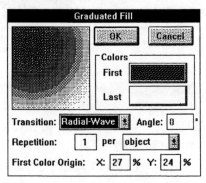

origination point to create your own graduated fill
style. The transition type and repetition style are
altered from combo boxes; the transition angle and
first colour origin can be altered either by entering
new values in the appropriate boxes or by dragging

the origination point (to set the origin) or moving the angle indicator. Clicking on either the First or Last Color panel brings up the Named colors dialog and lets you change the starting and finishing colours to any which are available from the colour selection.

Clicking on the Name button lets you save a fill style under its own name. This name will appear in the Styles list box.

Named Styles can also be accessed by choosing **Attributes/Styles...** and then **List/Fill**.

The fill style chosen with the Fill Attributes dialog will become the current fill style. The current fill style is displayed in the Fill Attributes Tool, and will be applied by default to all new objects. To apply the current fill style to any object, select the object by clicking on it and choosing **Attributes/Recall** (keyboard shortcut CTRL+R). Note: if you have saved another fill style using **Attributes/Save** (keyboard shortcut CTRL+Q), then the saved fill style will be applied instead.

# 9. Special Effects

## Blending

Blending is one of the new features in *Apprentice 1.1*. Blending is used to create special effects with multiple copies of the same object. Typically, blends are used to make a gradient or a gradual transition effect. Freeform objects, text and symbols can all be blended. The two objects at either end of the blend must be the same basic shape (you cannot change a circle into a square for example, or change text from one typeface to another), but the objects can be of different sizes, rotated or slanted, or have different colour and fill attributes.

To blend a piece of text, a symbol or freeform object, it must first be selected by clicking on it with the pointer. The next step is to choose **Manipulate/Blend...** which brings up the Blend

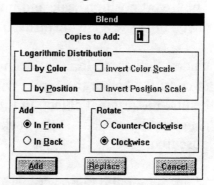

dialog. The blend dialog controls blending effects.

125

Enter the number of copies to add by entering a value between 1 and 99 in the Copies to Add box. If you choose a low number, it will be possible to see several distinct copies between the two end objects; if you choose a high number, the copies will overlap to a greater or lesser extent. The exact effect will depend on several things, including the distance between the end objects; the only way to find out what does and doesn't look good is to experiment.

Next, choose the type of Logarithmic Distribution (if any) which you want by checking the appropriate check box. The default is to have no boxes checked which gives a linear distribution with evenly spaced copies. A logarithmic position scale makes the copies near the final object more spread out than the copies near the first object. A logarithmic colour scale makes the copies near the final object change colour more rapidly than the copies near the first object.

The Invert position scale and Invert color scale check boxes reverse the distribution.

Choose either the In Front or In Back radio buttons to control whether the copies will be in front of or behind the original object. In Front results in the original object being at the back, i.e. partly obscured.

The Rotate radio buttons specify in which direction rotation should take place, in relation to the first object, if either of the objects has been rotated.

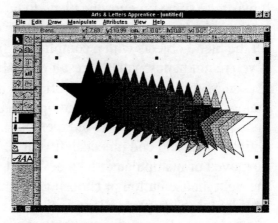

*Linear blend, copies in back, original on left*

Once the options have been specified, click on the
Add button. This adds a duplicate of the original
object to the page, which is selected and can be
moved and manipulated, or have its attributes
changed.

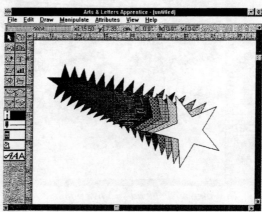

*Rotating clockwise and growing*

Once you have moved and altered the duplicate
object, choose **Manipulate/Complete Blend** or
click the right mouse button to complete the blend.

127

It may take some time for the blend to be drawn, particularly on slower PCs or if you have chosen to fill the blend objects with a complicated fill pattern. If you're not happy with the result of the blend, choose **Manipulate/Blend...** to bring up the Blend dialog again, respecify the blend options and click on the Replace button. The old blend disappears, with the start and end objects left visible. These can be moved or manipulated, if so desired. Clicking on the right mouse button or choosing **Manipulate/Complete Blend** will draw the new blend. If you click on the Add button instead of the Replace button, a new blend will be created with the new specifications, but the old blend will be left intact.

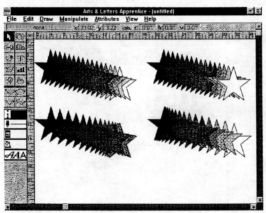

*The same basic blend - 15 five pointed stars, original (black) on left, final (white) on right - under different conditions. Upper left: linear blend, new copies in back; upper right: linear blend, new copies in front; lower left: logarithimic distribution by position; lower right: inverse logarithimic distribution by position*

# Binding text to shapes

Text can be bound to any freeform line, curve or object.

### Drawing a predefined curve for text binding

The Clip-Art manager contains a selection of predefined arcs and s-curves - the commonest shapes for text to be bound to - for you to use as this is more convenient than drawing a line by hand every time. To draw a predefined curve, access the Clip-Art Manager by choosing **Draw/Clip-Art Manager** (keyboard CTRL+C) or clicking on the Library tool.  In the list of Selected Clip-Art Libraries highlight *Curves for Binding Text. A range of curves and arcs appears in the Available Symbols list.

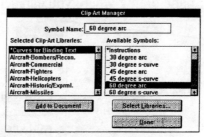

Highlight the curve or arc which you wish to use and add it to your design by clicking on the Add to Document button. The Object Adding tool appears on the screen and you can place the curve by clicking the left mouse button or dragging, as with any piece of Clip-Art. Remember that the pre defined shapes are freeform curves which can be edited in freeform editing mode.

## Drawing a freeform curve for text binding

Use the freeform curve drawing tool to draw a suitable curve, and edit it in freeform editing mode.

## Drawing a solid shape for text binding

Use the Add Symbol dialog to add a suitable symbol to the page. Convert it to a freeform shape by choocing **Draw/Cvt to Freeform** (keyboard shortcut F8) and edit the shape with the freeform editing tools.

## Binding the text to the shape

To actually create the effect, use shift-click or the block tool to select both the shape and the text which you wish to bind to it, and choose **Manipulate/Bind to Shape** to bring up the Bind to Shape dialog where you can set options for how you

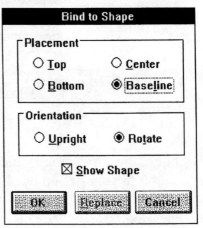

wish the finished effect to appear. The Placement radio buttons control which part of the text you wish to 'stick' to the shape. The default is Baseline:

130

the baseline of text is an imaginary line on which

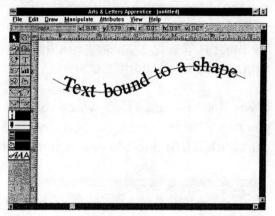

*The default - text rotated, on baseline, shape
visible*

the text sits with the tails of letters like g, y and q
hanging below it. The Orientation radio buttons
control whether the text should remain upright or
rotate to fit a tangent of the curve. Checking the
Show Shape check box means that the shape will be

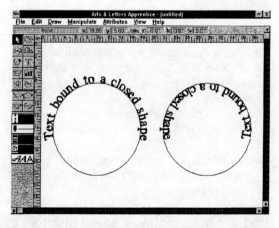

*Text bound to a closed shape (left) and the same
effect with the shape's Order of Points reversed*

displayed in the final effect and clearing it means that the shape won't be displayed. Click on OK to carry out the binding process. You can undo the binding process by choosing **Manipulate/Break Apart** (keyboard shortcut CTRL+U).

If you don't like the effect which you have created, you can alter the binding options by choosing **Manipulate/Bind to Shape...** again to redisplay the

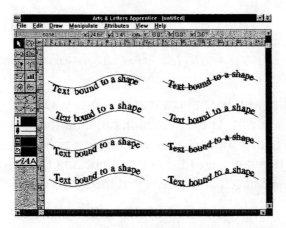

*Top Row. Left: Line Placement Top, Rotated text; Right: Line Placement Center, Rotated text.*
*Second Row. Left: Line Placement Bottom, Rotated Text, Right: Line Placement Baseline, Rotated Text.*
*Third Row. Left: Line Placement Top, Unrotated text; Right: Line Placement Center, Unrotated text.*
*Bottom Row. Left: Line Placement Bottom, Unrotated Text, Right: Line Placement Baseline, Unrotated Text.*

Bind to Shape dialog. Choose different options - for example you may decide not to display the shape -

and click on the Replace button to replace the old effect with the new one. Again, experimenting is the only way to find out which effects do and do not work.

Text which is bound to a shape can still be edited with the Text Entry/Editing dialog, have its type attributes changed via the Type Attributes dialog or have its line and fill attributes changed.

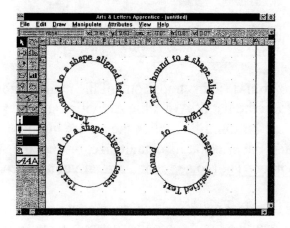

*Text bound to a shape with different alignments*

## Special text effects

Apprentice 1.1 features a number (21) of special text effects which are acessed via the Activity Manager. They are actually Warp Objects or similar objects which have been drawn with the more sophisticated facilities of the Arts & Letters Editor, but due to the close family relationship of

Apprentice and Editor, they can be manipulated in a limited way in Apprentice.

To use an effect, choose **Draw/Activity Manager...** and select the activity Text Effects. To add an effect

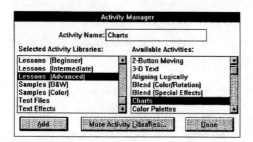

to your design, choose one of the named effects from the list of Available Activities and click on the Add button. Either click the mouse button once to add the effect at its default size, or drag the Add Object Tool to add it at a size of your choice.

The effect appears as a Group consisting of the effect itself and some instructions. Choose

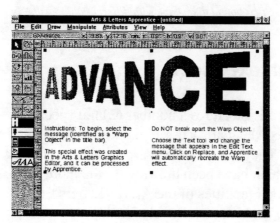

134

**Manipulate/Break Apart** to break the Group into two. Select and delete the **instructions only**.

The effect is now ready to use. Select it, and choose **Draw/Text...** or click on the Text Tool. Replace the text which appears in the Text Entry/Editing dialog with your own text and click on the Replace button. The effect will be redrawn using your own words.

You can alter the appearance of the text with the Text Attributes dialog, although you won't be able to change the text into a printer font. Because the effect is a single object, you can also slant, rotate or resize the effect. It's also possible to alter the text's fill and line attributes via the appropriate dialogs.

Note that if you use F8 to convert the effect to freeform and then ungroup it, all you will have is a collection of independent freeform objects.

# The Effects

**Advance**

**ADVANCE**

**Brick Walls**

**BRICK WALLS**

**Corkscrew**

**Curve**

**Curved Label**

**Drop Shadow**

**Drop shadow**

**Neon Lights**

# NEON
# LIGHTS

**Raised**

**Receding**

**Refection**

REFLECTION

**Rollercoaster**

**Rotate**

**Round 'n' Round**

**Rush**

## Shamrock

## Spin

## Spiral

**Steel Words**

**Underground**

**Wave**

**Wavey**

# 10. Charts

## General

Charts are usually a method of getting information across to people in a less intimidating and more easily understood way than a table with rows and columns of figures. A chart can emphasise those points to which you wish to draw attention, whilst obscuring information which is not so favourable. Apprentice lets you create charts for use in presentations or for pasting/exporting into other documents. A chart drawn with Apprentice can be used on its own, or combined with symbols and freehand objects as part of a bigger design.

## The Apprentice Chart Window

To draw a chart, it's necessary to access the Chart Window. Do this either by choosing **Draw/Chart...** or by clicking on the Chart Tool. The Chart

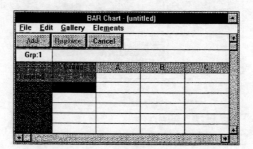

Window is a mini-application which runs within Apprentice. It has its own menus to access its

features and can be maximized or minimized. It can import and export data in several formats.

# The Chart Window Menus

### The File Menu
**File/Import...** brings up a dialog where you can choose to import data in a limited number of

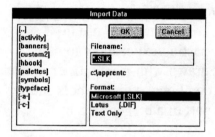

formats.
**File/Export...** brings up a dialog where you can choose to export data in a variety of formats.

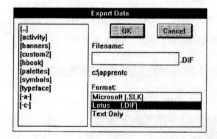

### The Edit Menu
**Edit/New** starts a new chart
**Edit/Cut** places the data from the currently selected cells on to the Clipboard

**Edit/Copy** places a copy of the data from the currently selected cells on to the Clipboard
**Edit/Paste** places a copy of the data from the Clipboard into the currently selected cells
**Edit/Clear Range** clears the currently selected cells
**Edit/Insert Row** inserts a new blank row above the current row
**Edit/Insert Column** inserts a new blank column to the left of the current column
**Edit/Delete Row** deletes the current row
**Edit/Delete Column** deletes the current column
**Edit/Column Width...** brings up a mini-dialog where you can specify the width (in characters) of the column.

## The Gallery Menu
The Gallery menu allows you to change the type of chart. You can choose from Area, Bar, Line, Pie and Point charts. The current chart type is checked and also appears in the Chart window's title bar.

## The Elements Menu
**Elements/Titles...** brings up a dialog where you can specify the Chart Title, X-Axis Title and Y-Axis title.
**Elements/Attributes...** brings up a dialog to specify, via sub dialogs, the attributes of chart elements.

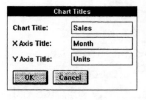 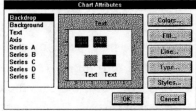

*The Chart Titles dialog (left) allows you to specify the titles
which will appear on the chart, and the Chart Attributes dialog
(right) allows you to specify the style of individual chart
elements*

**Elements/Y-Axis scale...** brings up a dialog to
specify the upper and lower limits which should be
shown on the Y-Axis (vertical scale).

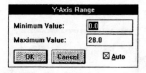

Display of various chart elements (Legend, Values,
BackGround, BackDrop and BackDrop Shadow)
can be turned off or on from this menu. Items which
will be displayed appear ticked in the menu.

# Buttons

The Chart Window has three buttons. Clicking on
the Add button adds a new chart to your design.
Clicking on the Replace button replaces the existing
chart with a modified one. Clicking on the Cancel
button closes the Chart window and returns you to
the main *Apprentice* program.

# The Data Area

The data area has seven columns and fourteen rows of which five columns (A-F) and 12 rows (1-12) (60 cells) can hold data. One column is used to hold Group names, and one row is used to hold a legend. You can use the scroll bars to view other parts of the data area, or click on the maximize button to view the whole data area at once.

# Creating a chart

Although you can import data, you can also enter it directly and this is what we'll do in this example. First of all, we need some data. Conveniently, the Chart window has 12 rows: one for each month We are going to show the year's sales for Woof-Woof dog food in each of four regions, in thousands of cases.

|           | North | South | East | West |
|-----------|-------|-------|------|------|
| January   | 25    | 26    | 20   | 19   |
| February  | 25    | 26    | 24   | 19   |
| March     | 25    | 26    | 23   | 20   |
| April     | 26    | 27    | 26   | 20   |
| May       | 26    | 24    | 25   | 21   |
| June      | 18    | 25    | 26   | 22   |
| July      | 27    | 26    | 25   | 25   |
| August    | 28    | 27    | 26   | 26   |
| September | 30    | 29    | 25   | 22   |
| October   | 28    | 27    | 26   | 21   |
| November  | 26    | 25    | 27   | 21   |
| December  | 24    | 25    | 28   | 22   |

When these figures have been entered into the data area, it looks like this:

| | | North | South | East | West |
|---|---|---|---|---|---|
| | January | 25 | 26 | 20 | 19 |
| | February | 25 | 26 | 24 | 19 |
| | March | 25 | 26 | 23 | 20 |
| | April | 26 | 27 | 26 | 20 |
| | May | 26 | 24 | 25 | 21 |
| | June | 18 | 25 | 26 | 22 |
| | July | 27 | 26 | 25 | 25 |
| | August | 28 | 27 | 26 | 26 |
| | September | 30 | 29 | 25 | 22 |
| | October | 28 | 27 | 26 | 21 |
| | November | 26 | 25 | 27 | 21 |
| | December | 24 | 25 | 28 | 22 |

The next step is to decide what kind of chart is required. In this example, it'll be a line chart, so choose **Gallery/Line**. The Titles are fundamental to understanding any chart. Choose **Elements/Titles...** to bring up the relevant dialog. In the Chart Title Box, enter Woof-Woof dogfood sales. In the X-Axis box, enter Month. In the Y-Axis box, enter Cases (000s). Click on OK. Next, choose **Elements/Attributes...** to specify the appearance of the chart elements: highlight an element in the list on the left and click one of the five rectangular buttons (Colors, Fill, Line, Type or Styles) on the right of the dialog to bring up further dialogs for changing that element's attributes. The changes are reflected in the preview shown in the middle of the dialog. For now, don't make any changes.

To place the chart in the design, click on OK. The mouse pointer changes to the add object tool; click the left mouse button once to add the chart at its default size, or drag the mouse to create a rectangle for it to flow into.

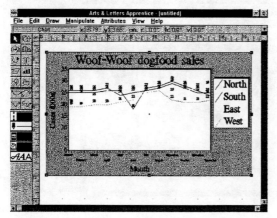

Once it has been placed in the design, the chart is a Group which can be moved or resized, rotated, slanted and so on. Choosing **Draw/Chart...** while the chart is selected will return you to the Chart Window where you can amend the chart - say by choosing a different style from the Gallery menu, or by removing one of the elements. The Replace button will now be ungreyed, and clicking on it will replace the old chart with the new one.

You can break the chart apart like any other Group, but once you've done this it will be just a collection of freeform and solid objects and you won't be able to edit via the Chart Window.

You can enhance the chart by adding symbols or pieces of clip-art. For example, you could add one or more of the dogs from the Nature - Cats and

147

Dogs Clip-Art library. Other objects could be added to emphasise particular points.

Be careful to choose an appropriate chart format. For example, if you choose **Gallery/Pie**, only the data from the first column will be used, resulting in this chart:

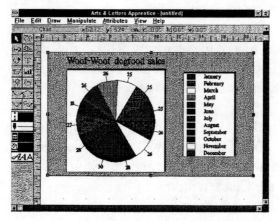

which is a month-by-month sales breakdown for the North region and does not enable a region-by-region comparison to be made.

148

Note that *Apprentice* doesn't support DDE
(Dynamic Data Exchange) or OLE (Object Linking
and Embedding) so you cannot make, for example,
data in a Microsoft Excel spreadsheet automatically
update an *Apprentice* design or vice versa.

The other major limitation of the Apprentice chart
drawing feature is that you are restricted to a small
data table of five columns by twelve rows. There is
however nothing to stop you drawing an elaborate
chart with Microsoft Excel or Lotus 1-2-3 for
Windows and importing it as a graphic via the
Windows Clipboard, although you won't be able to
break the picture apart and it will be in black and
white only.

# 11. Importing & Exporting

Each computer drawing package seems to have its
own proprietary file standard which can't be directly
used by any other package. Apprentice's GED format
can't be read by Corel DRAW! and Corel DRAW!'s
CDR format can't be read by Apprentice for example.
Yet these programs can create files which can be
read by each other and by many different Windows
and non-Windows programs too. These file formats
aren't the programs' 'native' formats but are
common standards, just as ASCII and RTF are used
by word processors and xBase is used by database
programs. Windows programs can additionally
communicate with each other via the Clipboard.

## Importing graphics files

To import a file created and saved with another
program into *Apprentice*, choose **File/Import...** to
bring up the Import filing dialog. Select the file
format of the file which you wish to import from the
list on the right. Because *Apprentice* only supports a
limited number of file formats, you may need to use
a graphics conversion program such as *Paint Shop
Pro* or *HiJaak!* to convert your graphic files to a
format which the program can read.

Select a file to import by highlighting its name and
clicking on the OK button, by double-clicking on its
name, or by typing its name in the Filename box.

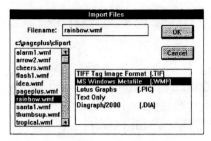

When you have done this, the pointer changes to the
Add Symbol tool. Click the mouse button once to
place the graphic at its default size with its top left
corner at the position of the mouse cursor or
click-drag to place the graphic at a size which you
think appropriate.

*Apprentice* refers to imported graphics as pictures.
You can't convert a picture to a freeform object, or
break it apart. As with Symbols and pieces of
Clip-Art, you can resize an imported graphic by

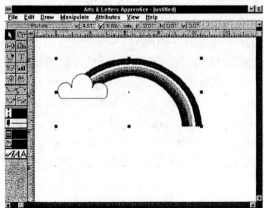

dragging on its edge or corner handles with the
mouse pointer.

152

Imported bitmaps cannot be rotated or slanted. If you do try and rotate a bitmap, the screen will display a grey bounding box with the file's name and all that will print will be a grey bounding box.

## Importing graphics via the Clipboard

In the 'other' application, select the item which you wish to export and choose **Edit/Copy** or use the keyboard shortcut CTRL+INS to place a copy of it on the Windows Clipboard. Change to *Apprentice*, and choose **Edit/Paste** or use the keyboard shortcut SHIFT+INS to place a copy of the object you have just placed on the Clipboard into *Apprentice*. Click once to place the object at its default size, or shift-drag to place the object at the size you choose.

## Exporting files in a foreign format

Other programs cannot directly use *Apprentice*'s ged files. You can export files in formats which other programs can use. To export a file choose **File/Export...** to bring up the Export dialog. Select either the Selected Objects or the Current Page radio button to decide which parts of the design to export. Choose the file format which you wish to export the objects to, and click on the Setup button to set the export options. See the *Import and Export Filters* appendix for a full list of formats and

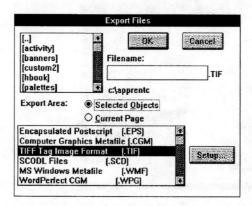

options.

Once you have chosen the export filter and set the options type the file's name in the Filename box and

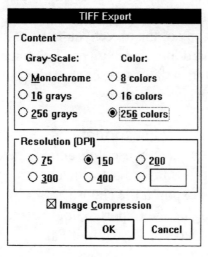

*This is the TIFF Export options box. All of the Export filters have option boxes, but they aren't all as comprehensive as this.*

click on OK to perform the export. Depending on
the filter and options chosen, the export file may be
**very** large and the process may take some time. The
Export Status box informs you of progress. Clicking
on the Cancel button stops the export process.
Cancelling an export will not erase the partially
created file; you will have to delete it from the File
Manager or DOS. If there is not enough free disk
space the export process will fail.

## Exporting graphics via the Clipboard
Select the objects which you wish to export, and
choose **Edit/Copy** or use the keyboard shortcut
CTRL+INS to place a copy of the selected object(s) on
the Windows Clipboard. Change to the other
Windows application, and choose **Edit/Paste** or use

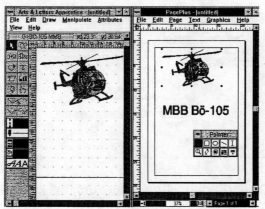

*A piece of Apprentice Clip Art pasted into a
PagePlus DTP document via the Clipboard*

155

the keyboard shortcut SHIFT+INS to place a copy into the other program using its rules for pasting graphics from the clipboard.

### Importing text from a file

Choose **File/Import...** and select the filter Text Only. Locate the text file which you wish to import, highlight its name and click on OK. Clicking the mouse button once will add the text to the design. Apprentice does not automatically word wrap. Unless the text includes carriage return/line feed symbols, it will be imported as one long line. Only import files which are in plain text format, as *Apprentice* has no filter for removing formatting commands inserted by word processing programs.

### Importing text via the Clipboard

You can import text into Apprentice from other Windows programs (for example, Windows Notepad) via the clipboard. To do this, in the

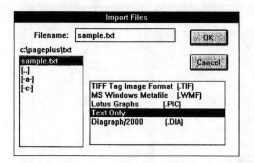

'other' application, select the text and use **Edit/Copy** (keyboard CTRL+INS) to put the text on the clipboard. Change to *Apprentice* and choose

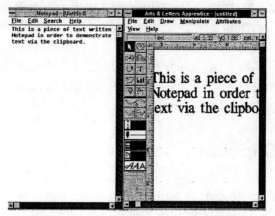

*Text pasted from Windows Notepad into
Apprentice*

**Edit/Paste** (keyboard SHIFT+INS) to paste the text
into the design.

*Apprentice* does not automatically word wrap and
just as with imported text, unless the text includes
carriage return/line feed symbols, it will be
imported as one long line.

## Exporting text

*Apprentice* does not have a filter to export text and
therefore if you wish to export text from Apprentice
to another application you have to do so via the
Clipboard.

Select the text string which you wish to export and
copy it to the Clipboard using **Edit/Copy** (keyboard
CTRL+INS). Change to the other application and paste

the text from the Clipboard using **Edit/Paste** (keyboard SHIFT+INS).

If you wish to save the text as a .TXT file, paste it into Notepad and save it via **File/Save As...** using a suitable filename.

## Clipboard Options

Choose **Edit/Clipboard...** to set the Clipboard Options, which control the way in which *Apprentice* communicates with the Clipboard and vice versa.

The Cut/Copy Formats section contains check boxes where you can specify what kind of image is on the page; the defaults are Arts & Letters and Windows Metafile; additionally you can choose Bitmap if there are bitmaps in the Arts & Letters design or if you want an *Apprentice* design or Metafile to be converted to a bitmap during cutting/copying.

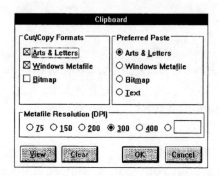

The Preferred Paste section contains radio buttons to control what type of image is pasted from the clipboard. Arts & Letters is the default, which should be used for pasting *Apprentice* designs into other programs. Windows Metafile should be chosen to export metafiles to other programs. Bitmap should be used if you are pasting bitmaps, and Text if you are pasting text.

You can also choose the paste resolution, and by clicking on the View button you can view the contents of the clipboard. Clicking on the Clear button clears the contents of the clipboard.

Setting the Clipboard options so that all the Cut/Copy check boxes are checked, and setting the Preferred Paste to Bitmap, copying an object to the Clipboard and pasting it into *Paint Shop Pro* or Windows *Paintbrush* is far quicker than using the TIFF filter to export a bitmap.

# 12. Printing

## Choosing and setting up your printer

### Choosing a printer

If you are lucky, you will be buying a new printer to use with *Apprentice* and Windows. In the real world, most of us aren't so lucky and will have to use an existing printer. If however, you are buying a new printer there are three major factors to consider: print method, type (colour/b&w) and cost.

**9 or 24 pin dot matrix printers** are relatively slow and very noisy, and are no good for producing finished output as the resolution is not high enough and the paper is inevitably dented by the impact of the pins. They are however quite happy to churn out paper year after year, and can print on multi-part and continous stationery. For drafting, they may be useful. Both black and white and colour dot matrix printers are available, at prices from £120 to £400 or more.

**Inkjet printers** spray minute droplets of ink from a specially designed print head onto the paper and deliver medium (300 dpi) resolution. Again, they're quite slow, but quiet. Against this, they can't handle multipart forms, the liquid ink can bleed into cheaper paper and running costs are high. Both black and white and colour inkjets are available, and the colour output can be superb. The cost varies from around £300 plus for a black and white printer, and upward of £500 for a colour printer.

**Laser and LED** printers use an electrostatic process similar to photocopying. Resolution is usually 300 dpi but 600 dpi printers are now appearing, and if you can afford one the output quality can be of near imagesetter quality. The two major standards are PCL (Hewlett Packard Printer Control Language) and PostScript, developed by Adobe. PostScript printers are more expensive but have the advantage of using the same commands as imagesetters. Laser and LED printers are easy to use, and cheap to run but relatively expensive initially. Colour laser printers are not yet in wide use. Black and white laser printers cost from £700 up for a reasonably specified machine.

**Thermal wax printers** deposit tiny blobs of molten wax onto special paper to build up their images. The results look fantastic, but the cost - both the capital outlay on the machine and the running cost per page are very high. The cheapest wax printers start at over £2000 with the cost-per-page at several pounds.

### Setting up your printer

To get the best results from your printer in combination with Windows and *Apprentice*, it should be set up with the Windows printer driver which is designed for your printer or the one recommended for it by the manufacturer. New printer drivers are released from time to time and are often available via bulletin boards or shareware libraries.

If you are using a laser printer, it should have at least 1.5MB and preferably more of RAM (on board memory). This will speed up the time that the printer takes to produce a page of output. More RAM on your PC will speed up Windows print spooler, the Print Manager.

Use a good quality paper and the apparent image quality may well improve; especially if you are using an inkjet printer, one of the specially treated papers will provide much better results as the ink won't bleed into the fibres.

## Setting up your page

Apprentice uses an invisible grid to determine the

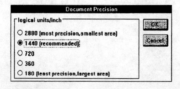

precision with which documents are sent to the printer. The greater the precision, the smaller the area which can be printed. The default setting of 1440 logical units per inch is suitable for most applications: you may want to increase it when producing slides for example or decrease it when printing large banners.

# Tiling

Apprentice allows you to produce tiled pages. This means that if your design extends over more than one page, you can choose All Pages in the Print dialog and your printer will print several pages each with part of the design on it which can then be manually assembled into one big sheet - a great way of producing banners for events. To make your printable area bigger, use the Document Precision option in the Page Setup dialog to reduce the document precision. As a rough guide, the default document precision of 1440 logical units per inch lets you have four A4 pages, equivalent to an A2 page. Reducing the document precision to 720 logical units per inch lets you print an area equivalent to five A4 pages wide and four A4 pages deep: at 180 logical units per inch (the lowest possible precision), you can print a tiled area equivalent to 22 A4 pages wide and 16 A4 pages deep!

Printing

Choose **File/Print...** to bring up the printing dialog. Choose whether to print All Pages, the Current Page or Selected items by selecting the appropriate radio button. If you are printing to a PostScript printer the Setup button in the PostScript section is ungreyed and leads to a further dialog for setting screen options. Click on Print to start printing. Clicking on the To File button directs output to a file instead of the printer port.

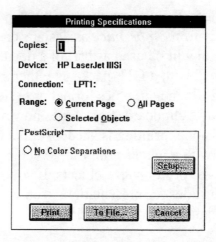

During printing, which may take some time, a

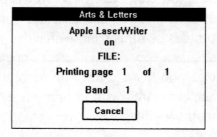

progress message is displayed.

# Postscript, bureaux and professional printing

## General

Postscript is the graphics and printing industries'
standard for computer-generated files. For most
uses, output from *Apprentice* or another package via
a laser printer or even a good ink jet printer
photocopied to make copies for distribution will be

sufficient. Very often, there will be no need to print directly from *Apprentice* as designs created with the program will be used as part of a document designed with a DTP package; either saved as an export file in a graphics format or pasted using the Windows clipboard. Sometimes however, professional printing is needed, either to keep costs down with a longer print run, to achieve special effects or print outsize objects. If you wish to make 35mm slides for presentations, you will have to use a specialist slidemaking service.

## Imagesetting Bureaux

One significant benefit of professional printing, particularly if you use a service bureau to make the bromides or films from which the printing plates are made, is a very much sharper appearance. Curves look smoother and have no perceptible 'jaggles' when compared with ordinary laser output. Text remains legible even at very small sizes (below 6 points).

Output bromides or films are made by imagesetters, which are very high resolution 'printers'. The image on the bromide or film is made up, according to the particular machine, of thousands of tiny dots at a rate between 1200 dpi and 2400 dpi. A standard laser printer typically prints at 300 dpi, and a dot-matrix printer at 180 dpi.

Because imagesetters are so expensive and specialised, the usual way to get the use of an imagesetter is to go to a service bureau. There are service bureaux in most large towns, and a look through the advertisment pages of almost any major computer magazine will yield the names of bureaux which accept work by mail (on disk) or via modem link.

Don't just pick a bureau from Yellow Pages or a magazine ad, give them your masterpiece and expect a magnificent result. Check them out first. Ask for information leaflets and details of previous work carried out for other clients. If they are local, ask if you can visit their premises and see samples of their current work. Find out how you will have to send the files. Is the bureau PC or Mac based? Do they run *Apprentice* themselves, allowing you to send a GED file on disk, or will you have to send a PostScript file? What kind of output do you require - bromide, positive film, negative film, right-reading or wrong-reading? Ask your printer. Find out the cost of extras, such as paper proofs, high-speed turnaround and delivery, as well as the cost per page of output. You may be able to make significant cost savings for example by using a slower delivery service. There's simply no point in overnight courier delivery at £30 a time if the job isn't really urgent and the same item could be sent via regular mail for £3 with delivery in 2-3 days. Note that *Apprentice* can't produce colour separated PostScript although it's possible to read a GED file compiled with *Apprentice* into the full-blown *Arts & Letters Graphics Editor*, which will produce separations. Some bureaux offer full-colour output on plain paper via a colour photocopier with a computer interface. Although very expensive, this may be a good solution if you only require a few copies.

A local bureau may appear more expensive than a postal-service bureau; there are advantages however, such as being able to deliver copy and pick up finished work in person and avoid delivery delays. If you're using a distant bureau, you will be charged if proofs are sent for approval by fax. With a local bureau, if things go wrong, you are also on the spot to try and sort them out. You will also be dealing with 'real' people; establishing a good working relationship with a local firm can have real advantages.

## 35 mm slides

Mac based bureaux won't be able to read GED files directly, and will require either Postscript files or SCODL (SCD) files. PC based bureaux may be able to accept GED files directly.

## What to tell the bureau

Make it as clear as possible what you want. Use the checklist below as a guideline.

**Name and subject of file**
**Type of file** -e.g. Postscript or *Apprentice*?
**Output medium** - bromide, negative or positive film, right or wrong reading?
**Number of copies required**
**Page size** - A2, A3, A4, A5, Letter, Legal, custom?
**Page orientation** - landscape or portrait?
**Number of pages**

**Crop Marks** - professional printers often print on oversize stock and cut to size using crop marks as a guide.
**Paper proofs** - supplying a paper copy of your design to the bureau can help to make clear exactly what you want.

Everything which you send to a bureau should be clearly identified: mark disk labels with the filename, your name, phone and fax numbers and whether or not you require the disk(s) to be returned; all other items should also be identifiable.

When you receive the camera ready copy or film, it should be handled as little as possible and with great care. Films and bromides are both easily damaged by fingermarks or scratches. *Never* write notes for the printer directly onto copy, even in the margins. Always write a separate note.

# Printing to a Postscript file

You must install the appropriate Postscript driver on your system (with Windows 3.1, install a specific driver - find out which driver your bureau prefers; if you can't the Agfa 9000 driver often gives good results).

If you're using TrueType fonts, they will have to be downloaded to the printer; use the Send to Printer As option in the Advanced Options section of the Printer Setup dialog o decide whether they should be downloaded as Adobe Type 1 (small sizes print as bitmaps, larger sizes as outline fonts) or Type 3 (all bitmaps). Set the printer timeout to a high value (e.g. 600 seconds) otherwise the printer may timeout after a few minutes inactivity.

To print an *Apprentice* design to a PostScript file, firstly have the design on screen. Secondly, choose **File/Printer Setup...** and select your chosen printer driver. If necessary, alter the page setup as well. The third stage is to choose **File/Print...** to access the Print dialog. Check the To File radio button. If you want to add a screen, click on the Setup button and enter the screen values. Click on OK to return to the main print dialog. *Note:* most of the time, this step can safely be left out. In fact, it's probably best left alone altogether. Click on OK to start printing. You will be prompted for the name of the file to which you wish to direct output. Enter it and click on OK. While the file is printing, Apprentice displays a progress message.

If you are sending the file to a bureau which is based on Apple Macintosh or UNIX computers, you will need to remove the CTRL-D characters which are the first and last characters of the file as the Mac sees them as end of file markers. Use Windows Notepad or another text editor to do this.

Small files can be sent to the bureau on 3½" disks; larger ones may have to be sent via modem.

With a bit of luck the end result of printing, either on your own printer or via a bureau will be a quality finished item which gives a good impression.

# Appendices, Bibliography, Index.

# Appendix A. Glossary of Windows and PC terms

**ASCII.** American Standard Code for Information Interchange. The lowest-common-denominator for electronic messages and documents.

**BIOS.** A PC's Basic Input Output System. The BIOS information is needed by the PC at power-on to get basic information about the system configuration. The main types of BIOS are genuine IBM, Phoenix and AMD. BIOS information is always supplied on a ROM chip.

**Boot.** Start a PC by switching it on (cold boot) or resetting it by pressing CTRL+ALT+DEL (warm boot).

**Bootable disk.** A disk containing the DOS command interpreter file, COMMAND.COM, which enables the PC to start up. Usually the boot information will be on a PC's hard disk, but it's always a good idea to keep a bootable floppy disk handy in case of disaster.

**Button.** Buttons appear in Windows dialogs. They are rectangular and have text on them 'Push' a button by clicking on it, and it will appear to move. Buttons usually either close dialogs or message boxes (OK and Cancel) or lead to further dialogs.

**Cache.** High speed memory used in some PCs to provide a buffer between the processor and slower memory or peripheral devices that would otherwise form a 'bottle-neck' slowing down the system to the speed of the slowest component. Hard disk caching attempts to predict the next request from the disk and read that area into memory in advance of the processor request.

**CD-ROM.** Compact Disc Read Only Memory. Data storage device based on Compact Disc technology. Capable of storing huge amounts of information on one disk in a read-only format.

**Check box.** Element in a Windows dialog. A check box is a square box used to turn an option on or off. Check boxes

173

are checked and unchecked by clicking the mouse pointer in them. A checked box has an x in it, and means that the option is on. An unchecked (empty) check box means that the option is off.

**Clicking**. Pressing and releasing the mouse button.

**Clock speed.** The speed at which a CPU operates. Expressed usually in MHz (MegaHertz).

**Combo box.** An item in a Windows dialog, with a down-arrow at the right hand end of the box. Clicking on the arrow drops down a list of available choices.

**COMMAND.COM**. The DOS command interpreter, which converts what you type on the keyboard into a form that the PC can use. If you delete this file, your PC won't respond: all you'll see is an error message.

**CPU**. Central Processing Unit. The 'brain' of a PC. CPU chips in PC terms mean the Intel 80x86 family of chips and compatible chips produced by other manufacturers (e.g. AMD, Cyrix): 8086, 80286, 80386SX and 80386DX, 80486SX, 80486DX and 80486DX2. The chips get progressively faster and more powerful.

**Dialog box**. Windows applications communicate with the user via dialogs. A dialog box may have a simple choice of OK, NO and CANCEL buttons to 'press' in response to a question, or may display various options which can be changed by the user.

**DOS**. Disk Operating System. The basic PC command language which most PCs use. The current (late 1992) versions are Microsoft's MS-DOS 5.0 and Digital Research's DR-DOS 6.0. **Dot Matrix Printer (DMP).** Printer which produces an image on the paper by striking pins in a pattern through an inked ribbon. The printhead usually has either 9 or 24 pins. Noisy, but cheap to run and reliable. Can also print multi-part stationery, e.g. invoices, which a laser or ink jet printer can't. Usually used for things like mailing labels or database listings.

**Double-clicking**. Pressing and releasing the mouse button twice in quick succession.

**Dragging.** Moving the mouse whilst holding the mouse button down.

**DTP.** Desktop Publishing. The use of a computer program to combine text and graphic elements and perform typographical operations for final output as a printed item. Popular DTP programs include *PageMaker*, *Ventura Publisher*, *PagePlus* and *Timeworks Publisher*.

**Filing Dialog.** The dialog which Windows applications display when you wish to save or open a file.

**Floppy Disk.** Disk of magnetic material enclosed in a flat plastic case, used for data storage and transfer as well as distribution of software. 5¼" disks have capacities of 360K, 640K or 1.2MB; 3½" disks have a capacity of 720K, 1.44MB or 2.88MB. 3½" disks have a rigid plastic case and a metal shutter to protect the disk material.

**Format.** (1) To prepare a disk to store data. A disk which has not been formatted can't be used. (2) Electronic coding applied to stored data, often proprietary to a program.

**GPF.** General Protection Fault. The Windows 3.1 equivalent of a UAE. GPFs only crash one application at a time and do not crash the entire system.

**GUI.** Graphical User Interface. Operating System in which the user communicates with the PC using a mouse to 'press' on-screen buttons, move items around and so on. Also known as a WIMP (Windows, Icons, Mouse, Point) system. First developed by Xerox at Parc (Palo Alto Research Center) and popularised by other companies. Windows is a GUI.

**Hard disk.** Mass storage device used in PCs to store programs and data. Consists of rigid plates coated with magnetic medium which spin at high speed and are read/written by retractable read/write heads on metal arms. Enclosed in a factory sealed unit. Early hard disks had capacities of 10MB or 20MB; today 85MB or 100MB is the norm and sizes up to 350MB are becoming common.

**Hardware.** The PC, monitor, printer and other physical devices which form part of a system.

175

**Icon**. Graphical representation of a program which appears on the screen when the program is inactive or minimized.

**Ink jet printer.** Printer in which the printed page is produced by spraying droplets of liquid ink at a sheet of paper as it moves past the print head. Quiet, high quality output; however if low-quality paper is used, the liquid ink may bleed into the fibres of the paper. Relatively inexpensive to buy, but moderate to high running cost. Colour ink jet printers are the most common means of getting reasonable (300 dpi) colour output.

**Laser Printer.** Printer which prints pages by using a laser beam to electrostatically charge a revolving drum in a process related to photocopying. The charged drum presses against a sheet of paper, and the charge is transferred to the paper. The charged part of the paper then attracts powdered ink (toner) which is sealed to the paper with a heating process. High quality output, but due to the relatively high cost mainly a business tool until now, although prices are falling fast.

**Maximize.** Make a Windows application expand to fill the whole display. There are two ways of doing this: either click on the up-arrow at the extreme right of the title bar, or using the keyboard press ALT, SPACEBAR, X.

**Menu**. List of options or commands within a program.

**Minimize.** Make a Windows application reduce in size so that it appears on screen as an icon. There are two ways of doing this. Either click on the down-arrow at the right of the title-bar, or using the keyboard press ALT, SPACEBAR, N.

**Modem.** Electronic device for conducting one PC to another via the public telephone network.

**Monitor**. The screen unit on which applications are displayed. The commonest display standards are VGA (*Video Graphics Array*) and SVGA (*Super VGA)*, which are medium resolution and really the minimum needed to run Windows effectively.

**Mouse Mat.** Small foam mat, covered with cloth or PVC which is placed by the side of the keyboard to run the mouse about on in preference to slippery desk surfaces.

**Mouse**. Arrangement of switches, wheels and a rotating ball enclosed in a plastic case attached to a PC via a cable, used to move the on-screen cursor and manipulate objects on the screen.

**PC**. Personal Computer. Originally a term used by IBM to describe their first desktop computer in 1981. Now a generic term for any desktop or portable micro running MS-DOS.

**PC/XT, PC/AT.** Developments of the original IBM PC.

**PostScript.** Page description language developed by Adobe Systems, used to send instructions to printers and image setters.

**Printer Driver.** The Windows printer drivers convert output from the Windows application (e.g. *Arts & Letters Apprentice*) into the control codes needed to make your printer produce finished images on the page. It is essential to use the printer driver which has been developed for your printer.

**Radio button.** Radio buttons appear in Windows dialogs, and are used to indicate mutually exclusive choices. It is not possible to check more than one radio button in the same section of a dialog.

**RAM.** Random Access Memory. (1) The chip memory into which a PC loads programs and performs calculations. RAM is measured in kilobytes (K) and megabytes (MB). 1 megabyte is equal to 1024 kilobytes. RAM from 0-640 K is known as base RAM; the 384 K from 460-1024K is known as upper memory, and anything above that is known as either extended RAM or expanded RAM according to how the PC's hardware and software 'sees' it. (2) Chip memory on a laser printer used to build up the page image before it is transferred to the paper and to hold soft fonts.

**ROM.** Read Only Memory. A type of data storage from which data can be read, but not written to in modified form.

**Scanner.** Hardware for converting drawn or printed images to electronic form. Can be either hand held, or flatbed. Flatbed scanners can scan a bigger area and some can be left to run unattended, but they are much more expensive than a hand held scanner.

**System Unit.** The part of a PC, usually separate from the monitor, where the hard disk, floppy disk, CPU and associated electronics are located.

**TrueType.** Scalable font technology used by Microsoft Windows 3.1.

**UAE.** Unrecoverable Application Error. Windows 3.0 error message. If you see this message, your application has crashed. Exit Windows, reboot, and start Windows again.

**Virus.** Software written with malicious intent to destroy or corrupt data on the victim's PC. Often triggered by a particular date, e.g. Friday 13th. Viruses are self replicating, and often attach themselves to the boot sectors of a hard disk, infecting any floppy disks formatted from the affected machine Often distributed unintentionally by infected floppy disks being used to transfer programs from machine to machine.

**WIMP.** Window, Icon, Mouse, Pointer: another term for a Graphical User Interface (GUI).

**window.** Portion of the screen displaying part of a program.

**Windows.** Microsoft Windows graphical user interface.

**WYSIWYG.** Optimistic acronym for a program where What You See (on screen) is (almost the same as) What You Get (on paper).

# Appendix B. Glossary of Apprentice and Typographical Terms

**Accent.** (1) Marking placed above, below or through a letter to indicate pronunciation, for example *ü* (u-umlaut) in German is pronounced as "ue"; *ç* (c-cedilla) in French is pronounced like "s". Also known as *diacritical marks*. (2) In *Apprentice*, a symbol which, when placed on another symbol, transforms it from one thing to another.

**Alignment.** How objects appear relative to one another or to the page.

**ATM.** Adobe Type Manager. Font rendering software produced by Adobe Systems which allows PostScript outline fonts to be displayed on Windows-equipped PC screens and printed on any Windows-supported printer.

**Baseline.** The imaginary line upon which a line of text sits. Descenders, e.g. the tail of the letter *q* hang below the baseline.

**Bézier Curve.** Basically, a nice way of drawing smooth curves. A Bézier curve is a curve which follows a path defined by a series of control points. It is smooth and continuous and therefore ideal for computer drawing applications.

**Bitmap.** A graphic item made up of many tiny dots, often called a paint-type graphic: created by programs such as *PC Paintbrush*, *Windows Paintbrush*, or by scanners.

**Blackletter.** Fonts which resemble the script in use in the 15th century, e.g. Marigold or Garlic from LaserGo Inc.'s Type Commander collections. Also known by their German name of *Fraktur fonts*.

**Bold.** Font in which the type is heavier than the other fonts of the same typeface; often used for **emphasis**.

**Bullet.** Symbol used to draw attention to the start of a line or paragraph.

**Colour Models.** Colours are expressed as a mixture of different colours. The two main models are RGB in which colours are expressed as proportions of **R**ed, **G**reen and **B**lue; and CMYK in which the colours are expressed as proportions of **C**yan, **Y**ellow, **M**agenta and **K**ey. The Key is invariably black. RGB is appropriate for screen images, whereas CMYK is the standard for printing.

**Em.** The Em is proportional to the size, in points, of the font in use. An Em in a 36 point font will therefore be 36 x 36 points or ½ inch x ½ inch. In an 18 point font an Em will be 18 points x 18 points or ¼ inch by ¼ inch.

**En.** Half the width of an Em.

**Font.** A set of characters of the same general appearance and weight described by a distinctive name. Font does *not* mean the same as typeface.

**Italic.** Font in which the characters *slope to the right*. Typically the angle is around 15 degrees. Apprentice lets you change the italic angle of its own typefaces.

**Kerning.** Increasing or decreasing the space between pairs of letters to improve their appearance on the printed page.

**Landscape.** Page which is wide, that is with long sides at top and bottom and short sides at left and right.

**Object.** Any item placed on the workspace. Objects can be text or graphics.

**Pica.** Unit of measurement used by printers and designers. There are 6 picas per inch.

**Point.** Unit of measurement for type. There are 72 points per inch.

**Portrait.** Page which is upright, that is with short sides at top and bottom and long sides at the left and right.

**Typeface.** A collection of fonts in which all the characters look broadly similar. Times New Roman is a typeface which consists of four fonts: Times New Roman, **Times New Roman Bold**, *Times New Roman Italic*, and ***Times New Roman Bold Italic***.

# Appendix C. System Requirements, Setup and Optimisation

## System Requirements

*Arts & Letters Apprentice* is a Windows program, and so your PC must be capable of running Windows 3.0 or Windows 3.1; this means a PC with an 80286, 80386SX, 80386, 80486SX, 80486DX or 80486DX2 (or compatible) CPU, a hard disk, at least 2MB of RAM, and a VGA or better monitor. A Windows-supported printer is virtually essential ,as is a mouse or other pointing device.

As with all Windows programs, *Apprentice* will run more smoothly if your PC has a higher specification. If your PC has only the minimum requirements, *Apprentice* will slow to a crawl, particularly when redrawing objects with complex fill patterns like radial gradients.

**More RAM** is the easiest upgrade option for most newer PCs. SIMMs (Single In-line Memory Modules) can be bought and simply plugged in to the appropriate slot in the circuit board. Add as much as you can afford or as much as your system will support. Aim for at least 4MB.

**A fast hard disk** with a good caching controller will speed up disk-intensive operations considerably.

**A Video Accelerator Card** takes the processing of the screen image away from the CPU and therefore if one is fitted screen redraws will be much faster.

181

The three options listed above are all perfectly feasible as upgrades to an existing PC. However, if you are buying a new PC, having them installed by the manufacturer will be cheaper than adding them later.

**Important Warning:** Before undertaking any hardware upgrades yourself, make sure that you know exactly what you are doing. *A mistake could lead to irreparable damage to your PC and even personal injury.* If you are doubtful about any aspect of hardware upgrading, consult a qualified computer engineer.

**Optimising DOS and Windows**

DOS and Windows both impose their own ways of working on your PC. The two main versions of DOS in use at the time of writing (late 1992) are MS-DOS 5.0, a Microsoft product, and DR-DOS 6.0, a Digital Research product. DR-DOS 6.0 includes a version of SuperStor, a utility which increases the amount of data you can store on your hard disk, sometimes effectively doubling its size. If you are using an earlier version of DOS, seriously consider upgrading.

**Windows 3.1** is the version of Windows which is currently available. You may still have the older Windows 3.0, and although *Apprentice* will work with it, Windows 3.1 offers many improvements and you should consider upgrading.

When you switch on, DOS runs two configuration files which tell it about the resources which your PC has and the way in which it should use those resources. These files are called AUTOEXEC.BAT and CONFIG.SYS. How you set them up can materially affect how your PC performs. Sample

CONFIG.SYS and AUTOEXEC.BAT files for MS-DOS 5.0/Windows 3.1 are given below.

**Caution:** *before modifying CONFIG.SYS or AUTOEXEC.BAT, make sure that you have a bootable floppy disk (system disk) to hand, as a mistake in either of these files could lock up your system.*

MS DOS 5.0 + Windows 3.1

AUTOEXEC.BAT

```
@ECHO OFF
C:\WINDOWS3\SMARTDRV.EXE
PROMPT $p$g
PATH=C:\WINDOWS3;C:\DOS;C:\;
SET TEMP=C:\SCRATCH
SET DIRCMD = /O:N /P
LOADHIGH DOSKEY /BUFFSIZE=512 /INSERT
C:\DOS\KEYB UK,437,c:\DOS\KEYBOARD.SYS
```

CONFIG.SYS

```
FILES=50
BUFFERS=15
LASTDRIVE=E
STACKS=9,256
DOS=HIGH,UMB
DEVICE=C:\WINDOWS3\HIMEM.SYS
DEVICE=C:\WINDOWS3\EMM386.EXE NOEMS
DEVICEHIGH=C:\DOS\SETVER.EXE
-SHELL=C:\COMMAND.COM C:\ /E:512 /p
DEVICE=C:\DOS\MOUSE.SYS /Y
COUNTRY=44,437,C:\DOS\COUNTRY.SYS
```

DOS=HIGH, UMB must be before
DEVICE=C:\DOS\HIMEM.SYS,

SETVER can be loaded with DEVICEHIGH to save standard memory, SET TEMP should point to a specific temp directory and most importantly DOSSHELL should not be used.

The DOS pretender commands - APPEND, SUBST, JOIN (or similar utilities) should not be used.

**win.ini**

win.ini is the file which controls Windows applications. When Apprentice is installed for the first time, it creates a section called [a&l]which you can edit by hand if need be. Apprentice's install routine also adds a line to the [extensions] section of win.ini to associate ged files with Apprentice. This means that if you double-click on a ged file's name in the File Manager, Apprentice will automatically start up, with that file loaded. If you wnt this autostarting to apply to all ged files on any drive or path, it's necessary to add the directory which contains A&L_APPR.EXE to the path statement in autoexec.bat. After changing autoexec.bat, reboot you PC.

**Run Apprentice as your main Windows application**

If you always, or almost always, run Apprentice when your PC is turned on, you can set *Apprentice* to start automatically when Windows is invoked.

There are two ways of doing this.

1. in the [Windows] section of win.ini add a line reading

run=c:\apprentc\a&le_appr.exe or

2. drag the *Apprentice* icon into the Program Manager's StartUp group.

**Apprentice as a slideshow**

You can set up Apprentice to show a series of ged files
one after another in the manner of a slide show. This is
particularly useful if you are at an exhibition or wish to
leave a PC with a series of messages in a shop window for
example. In order to make these self running demos, you
need to modify win.ini.

In the [a&l] section of win.ini, add the following:

```
NumberOfLines=value
Filen=filename
Timen=time
Repeat
```

value is the number of files in the demo;
filename is the name and path of the ged file to display
timen is the time in seconds to open the file for.

**Add other programs to the system menu**

All Windows programs have a system menu which is the
small horizontal bar at the top right of the program
window. It is accessed by clicking on it, or by using the
keyboard combination ALT,SPACEBAR. Normally the only
choices available are Maximize, Minimize, Close, Restore
and Switch to... . Apprentice lets you add programs to
these choices, if you wish. To add programs, again you
need to edit win.ini. In the [a&l] section of win.ini, add
the line
```
programs=number
```
where the number is the number of programs to appear in
the menu. Next, add the name and path of each program
which you wish to add, e.g.

```
ProgramName1=Filer
ProgramPath1=file2.exe
```

To add the Windows Notepad and Paintbrush accesories, the new lines in win.ini would look like:

```
Programs=2
ProgramName1=Notepad
ProgramPath1=c:\windows\notepad.exe
ProgramName2=Paintbrush
ProgramPath2=c:\windows\pbrush.exe
```

Typical hardware for running Arts & Letters -
a 386 PC and laser printer

# Appendix D. Apprentice Import and Export filters

Arts & Letters Apprentice stores designs using .GED (*Graphic Environment Document*) file descriptions, also used by Arts & Letters Illustrator and Arts & Letters Editor. Strictly speaking, this is not a file format, as its name implies. Rather, it is a description of the page which tells *Apprentice* to get a certain combination of symbols from the symbol and clip-art libraries and place them on the page at certain positions, and also descriptions of the position and attributes of freeform objects. If a .GED file is loaded and *Apprentice* cannot locate symbols or typefaces included in the design, squares or rectangles will be displayed in place of the missing symbols.

In order to communicate with other programs, Apprentice has the facility to both import and export files in various formats.

## Import filters

| Extension | Type | Remarks |
|---|---|---|
| TIF | Tagged Image Format File | Bitmap graphics file format. The only bitmap file format supported by *Apprentice*. Compressed variants of TIFF files cannot be imported. |
| WMF | Windows Metafile | Draw (vector) graphics file format, used by many Windows applications |
| PIC | Lotus Graphs picture file | Picture file format used by Lotus 1-2-3 |
| *.* | Text Only | ASCII text files |
| DIA | Diagraph/2000 | File format used by some slide-making equipment |

## Export filters

187

| Name | Format | Description | Options |
|---|---|---|---|
| EPS | Encapsulated PostScript | PostScript output files | *Format:* Standard EPS or Adobe Illustrator<br>*Screen Image:* WMF or TIFF<br>Resolution: 75, 150, 200, 300, 400 or user specified dpi |
| CGM | Computer Graphics Metafile | Colour Metafile (draw) format | *Formats:* 16 Colour, Direct (16 million colours (24-bit))<br>*Resolution:* 75, 150, 200, 300, 400 or user specified dpi |
| TIF | Tagged Image Format File | Bitmap format | *Grey-scale:* Monochrome, 16 or 256 greys<br>*Colour:* 8, 16 or 256 colour<br>*Resolution:* 75, 150, 200, 300, 400 or user specified dpi |
| SCD | SCODL | Matrix Export Format for 35mm slide making machines | Number of Copies<br>Use Page Background Colour<br>TT200 Printer<br>*Resolution:* 200 or 400 dpi (2000 or 4000 lines) |
| WMF | Windows Metafile | Vector (draw) format for Windows Applications | *Resolution:* 75, 150, 200, 300, 400 or user specified dpi |
| CGM | WordPerfect CGM | Vector (draw) format for use by WordPerfect and related programs | *Resolution:* 75, 150, 200, 300, 400 |

**Export files generated using this option - especially colour TIFF files - can be very large and the export process can take a long time.**

188

# Appendix E. Apprentice Typefaces

Apprentice comes with a range of scalable typefaces. Most of these are generally similar to other commercially available typefaces whose names may be more familiar.

Knowing these names can be useful, for example if you wish to create a text effect which complements the main body of text in a DTP document.

| Apprentice Name | Ref | Equivalent Name |
|---|---|---|
| Artesia | 37 | Lubalin |
| Avondale Book | 76 | ITC Avant Garde |
| Avondale Bold | 79 | ITC Avant Garde Bold |
| Belvedere Medium | 79 | Benguiat Book |
| Cafe Demi | 61 | Peignot Bold |
| Classic Medium | 14 | Times Roman |
| Classic Bold | 15 | Times Roman Bold |
| Classic Heavy | 16 | Times Roman Heavy |
| Footlights | 32 | Broadway |
| Kaboose | 31 | Kabel |
| Memento | 41 | Souvenir |
| Modern Light | 20 | Helvetica Light |
| Modern Medium | 2 | Helvetica |
| Modern Bold Condensed | 25 | Helvetica Bold Condensed |
| Modern Heavy | 27 | Helvetica Inserat |
| Nonchalant | 87 | Dom Casual |
| Parchment | 49 | Uncial |

| Apprentice Name | Ref | Equivalent Name |
|---|---|---|
| Quadrille | 35 | Fritz Quadrata |
| Shadow | 94 | Umbra |
| Southwest | 46 | Capone Medium |
| Typewriter | 36 | American Typewriter |
| Urbanite Medium Extended | 18 | Eurostile Extended |
| Verona Medium | 51 | Bodoni |
| Verona Poster | 53 | Bodoni Poster |
| Wyeth | 50 | Brush Script |
| Ziegfeld | 68 | Revue |

As well as its own typefaces, *Apprentice* can make use of any fonts available to the selected printer. This means that fonts which have ben added with Adobe Type Manager, Windows 3.1 TrueType or another font manager can be used. However, you cannot apply different fill styles to text which is in a third-party font, nor can third-part typefaces be converted to freeform objects.

Further fonts in Arts & Letters format can be obtained from Computer Support Corporation or its representative (in the UK, contact The Roderick Manhattan Group).

# Appendix F. Command Reference

## Keyboard Shortcuts

| Key combination | Command |
| --- | --- |
| ALT+BKSP | Undo |
| CTRL+1 | view actual size |
| CTRL+2 | view current page |
| CTRL+3 | view all pages |
| CTRL+4 | view control points |
| CTRL+6 | show outlines only |
| CTRL+A | select all |
| CTRL+B | block select |
| CTRL+C | access clip-art library |
| CTRL+F | bring to front |
| CTRL+G | group |
| CTRL+I | fill attributes |
| CTRL+INS | copy |
| CTRL+K | send to back |
| CTRL+L | line attributes |
| CTRL+N | align |
| CTRL+P | enter/leave freeform editing mode |
| CTRL+Q | save current attributes |
| CTRL+R | recall saved attributes |
| CTRL+S | draw symbol |
| CTRL+T | enter/edit text |
| CTRL+U | ungroup |
| CTRL+V | show previous view |
| CTRL+X | view full screen |
| CTRL+Y | text attributes |
| CTRL+Z | zoom |
| DEL | delete |

191

| | |
|---|---|
| F1 | access help menu |
| F2 | draw line |
| F3 | draw curve |
| F5 | add handle |
| F7 | join open shapes |
| F8 | convert to freeform |
| F9 | Save |
| SHIFT+DEL | cut |
| SHIFT+INS | paste |
| TAB | fill attributes |

# Appendix G. Sources

Listed below are some sources for more information and useful add-ons (both software and hardware) to make using Arts & Letters Apprentice easier.

**The Roderick Manhattan Group,** Cloisters Business Centre, 8 Battersea Park Road, London, SW8 4AA. *Telephone 071-978 1727 (Technical Support 071-978 1737), Fax 071-622-2974.* UK distributor of Arts & Letters Apprentice and other Windows programs; technical support for Apprentice; source for add-ons/upgrades.

**Computer Support Corporation,** 15926 Midway Road, Dallas, TX 75224, United States of America. *Telephone +1 (214) 661-8960, Fax +1 (214) 661-5429.* Developer of Arts & Letters Apprentice and other programs.

**Third Party Products**

Before buying any new hardware or software products, it's always worth having a look through some of the specialist computer magazines for reviews and pricing. Prices can vary considerably, and you should never have to pay the full manufacturer's list price for things like software or laser printers. Below is a list, in alphabetical order of some of the many computer magazines available at the time of writing (late 1992). You should be able to get most of these titles from any multiple newsagent, or by order from your local newsagent.

Business Computing, Byte, Computer Shopper, PC Direct, PC Plus, PC Magazine, PC Today, PC Answers, Personal

Computer World, Which Computer, Windows Magazine, Windows User.

Some of the magazines have floppy disks of useful software (usually shareware or demo versions of commercial packages) attached; they are aimed at different parts of the personal computer market with some being very much business oriented whilst others are more general in their appeal.

**Paint Shop Pro.** A bitmap viewing, conversion and screen grabbing program. Converts virtually any bitmap graphics format to any other, including to/from TIFF. Published by JASC Inc., represented in the UK by The Thomson Partnership, Church Croft, Bramshall, Uttoxeter, Staffordshire, ST14 5DE. Telephone 0889 564601.

# Bibliography

Austin, Mike. **The ISTC Handbook of Technical Writing & Publication Techniques** *(2nd edition). ISTC/William Heinemann Ltd, London 1990.* ISBN 0 950 6459 23

Collier, David. **Collier's Rules for Desktop Design and Typography**. *Addison-Wesley, London 1991.* ISBN 0 201 54416 4.

Holme, C. (Editor). **The Art of the Book**. *Studio Editions Ltd., London 1990.* ISBN 1 85170 445. *(Facsimile of same book originally published 1914 by The Studio Limited, London.)*

Hunt, Richard. **PagePlus Illustrated**. *Kuma Computers Ltd, Pangbourne 1992.* ISBN 0 7457 0062 4.

Kleper, Michael L. **The Illustrated Handbook of Desktop Publishing and Typesetting** (2nd edition). *Windcrest/McGraw-Hill, 1990.* ISBN 0 8306 3350 2.

Utvitch, Michael. **The Official Arts & Letters Handbook**. *Bantam Books, New York 1991.* ISBN 0 553 35243 1.

White, Jan V. **Graphic Design for the Electronic Age**. *Watson Guptill, New York, 1988.*

# Index